AF600637

THE SPIRITUAL PREFECT IN CLERICAL RELIGIOUS HOUSES OF STUDY

THE CATHOLIC UNIVERSITY OF AMERICA
CANON LAW STUDIES
No. 216

THE SPIRITUAL PREFECT IN CLERICAL RELIGIOUS HOUSES OF STUDY

AN HISTORICAL SYNOPSIS AND COMMENTARY

BY

REV. NICHOLAS GILL, C.P., J.C.L.
PRIEST OF THE PROVINCE OF SAINT PAUL OF THE CROSS

A DISSERTATION

SUBMITTED TO THE FACULTY OF THE SCHOOL OF CANON LAW OF THE CATHOLIC UNIVERSITY OF AMERICA IN PARTIAL FULFILLMENT OF THE REQUIREMENTS FOR THE DEGREE OF DOCTOR OF CANON LAW

THE CATHOLIC UNIVERSITY OF AMERICA PRESS
WASHINGTON, D. C.
1945

Imprimi Potest:
CARROLUS RING, C.P.

Nihil Obstat:
HIERONYMUS D. HANNAN, A.M., LL.B., S.T.D., J.C.D.
Washingtonii, die 28 maii, 1945.

Imprimatur:
✠MICHAEL J. CURLEY, D.D.
Baltimorae, die 28 maii, 1945.

MURRAY & HEISTER—WASHINGTON, D. C.
PRINTED IN UNITED STATES

9

TABLE OF CONTENTS

PART ONE

HISTORICAL SYNOPSIS

PART TWO

CANONICAL COMMENTARY

FOREWORD

One of the most important works of the Catholic Church is the preparation of young men for the priesthood. The religious cleric must be given a proper intellectual education and a sound spiritual training. The latter task is entrusted to the Spiritual Prefect who continues the work begun in the novitiate by the Master of novices.

The present study is an attempt to trace the historical development of the office and function of the religious to whom the spiritual care of the students was entrusted at different periods of the Church's history, and to present a canonical commentary on the juridic institute known as the Spiritual Prefect. An investigation will be made concerning the nature of his office, his duties, his qualities, and other intimately related questions.

The present study is concerned principally with the office of the Spiritual Prefect as it is governed by the common law of the Code; it also considers the possibility and implications of the case in which the external discipline is joined, as in some institutes, to the function of the spiritual training of the students, and it lays down general principles governing problems arising out of the authority thus annexed to the office. The office of the Spiritual Prefect does not exist in all religious institutes, but only in those institutes, exempt or non-exempt, pontifical or diocesan, in which religious are prepared for the priesthood. It concerns only the clerics of religious institutes, and not clerics of the diocese who receive their training from religious in religious houses or in a seminary attached to a religious house. Moreover, the consideration of this office as related to societies of men living in common without public vows is not included in this study.

The duties assigned to the Spiritual Prefect in one community may be greater than those entrusted to him in another. Therefore the writer will constantly make reference to the scope of the office of Spiritual Prefect according to the common law, distinguishing it from the scope of the office according to the particular law. The particular application, then, will need to be made in each institute according to the nature of the office in that institute. Finally, whenever reference in this work is made to clerical religious, it means to include all who have made religious profession and are engaged in studies in a religious house of studies even though they have not yet received tonsure.

The writer takes this occasion to express his sincere appreciation to all those who have aided him in any manner in the preparation of this study. Particular gratitude is due to his Congregation, especially to the Very Rev. Carrol Ring, C.P., Provincial of the Province of St. Paul of the Cross, for the opportunity which has been afforded to the writer to pursue advanced studies in Canon Law, and to the Faculty of the School of Canon Law of the Catholic University of America for their considerate and generous assistance at all times.

CHAPTER I

THE AUTHORITY OF RELIGIOUS SUPERIORS

ARTICLE I. JURSDICTION AND DOMINATIVE POWER

A. AUTHORITY IN GENERAL

Societies as well as individuals have an aim to attain. Moral persons, just as physical persons, have their purpose for existing. That purpose may arise from the very nature of the society, or it may have its origin in some voluntary agreement on the part of those establishing the society, or it may be determined by a higher authority than itself. The aim of the society may be very general or very specific; but it is an end that is common to all the members that constitute the society.

Moreover, it is not sufficient simply that the aim of the society be clearly revealed to the members. Something further is required, since those making up the society are human beings weakened by original sin. Consequently, there must be authority, which in an official manner directs the subjects to the common end, and enforces the laws by proportionate sanctions.

The nature of the authority follows from the nature of the society.[1] If the society is one that arises from the very law of nature, for instance the state, then the extent of the authority will depend upon the extent of power needed officially to direct the society to its common end. On the other hand, a society founded by a group of individuals will have as much authority as the members voluntarily vest in the head.

The Church constitutes a perfect society, established by Jesus Christ and having as its ultimate purpose the salvation of souls. Its power is twofold, the power of orders and the power of juris-

[1] Ottaviani, *Institutiones Iuris Publici Ecclesiastici* (2 vols., 2. ed., Civitate Vaticana: Typis Polyglottis Vaticanis, 1935–1936), I, n. 120. Hereafter cited as *Institutiones*.

diction. Through the power of orders the Church is able to perform acts of divine worship and to administer the sacraments for the sanctification of the baptized. By means of jurisdiction the Church governs its subjects, authoritatively directing them in matters of faith, morals, and discipline to their final end.

In this perfect society—the Church—are found lesser societies, which are imperfect inasmuch as they do not have all the means in themselves of attaining their purpose. Among them are those called religious institutes. Each of these lesser societies has its own proper end, which however is not contrary to the ultimate end of the Church, but subordinate to it and dependent on the Church for regulation.

The authority exercised by the Church is called jurisdiction; the authority exercised in religious institutes, inasmuch as they are religious institutes, is called dominative power. Some religious institutes also have a share in the public power of the Church. Hence, since these terms occur constantly throughout this work, it is necessary to follow briefly the history of jurisdiction and dominative power, and to note the distinction between them today.

B. JURISDICTION

1. *History*

In the present canonical terminology power includes the power of *jurisdiction* and the power of *orders.*[2] The power of *orders,* granted to validly ordained ministers, has as its end the sanctification of the faithful through the conduct of divine worship and through the administration of the sacraments.[3] The power of *jurisdiction* is the public power of ruling the Church.[4] Since jurisdiction is a public power which is shared in by exempt religious institutes, it is necessary to examine briefly the term "jurisdiction" to discover if the word has changed in meaning in the centuries during which it has been used by the Church.

---

[2] Canons 145, § 1; 196; 210.

[3] Chelodi, *Ius de Personis iuxta Codicem Iuris Canonici* (ed. altera a Sac. Ernesto Bertagnolli recognita et aucta, Tridenti: Libr. Edit. Tridentum, 1927), n. 125. Hereafter cited as *Ius de Personis.*

[4] Chelodi, *Ius de Personis,* n. 125.

The Romans admitted a fourfold power in the state: *maiestas, imperium, iurisdictio* and *notio*. *Maiestas* was the supreme power which originally was vested in the people, and, later was transferred to the Emperor during the days of the Monarchy, and to the consuls at the time of the Republic. It was the supreme power, the font of all others. *Imperium* was the power of coercing criminals, or the power of the sword. *Iurisdictio* was the power of judging in contentious and civil cases, and of executing the sentence. *Notio* was the simple power of judging without the authority to execute the judgment.[5]

All these powers were exercised by the Emperor in the period of the Monarchy.[6] When the Monarchy gave way to the Republic the consuls continued to fulfill the powers and prerogatives of the kings.[7] However, during the reign of the consuls the office of praetor was established. It was the duty of the praetor to decide contentious cases, that is, to give a decision, and to see that the sentence was executed.[8] To the time of Justinian (527–565) the concept of jurisdiction retained the same meaning. "*Ius dicere*" was to render a decision in a judicial manner, to speak that which was just.

However, at the time of Justinian, when there was a mutual influence between canon and civil law, it seems that the term jurisdiction broadened in its scope to include more than judicial power. The term jurisdiction occurs in two of the Novels of Justinian, where it has the sense of a general authority which extends even to the administration of temporal matters.[9] This

[5] Raus, *De Sacrae Obedientiae Virtute et Voto secundum Doctrinam* Divi Thomae et S. Alphonsi, iuxta Normas ac Codicem Iuris Canonici (2 vols. in 1, Lugduni, Lutetiae Parisiorum: apud Emmanuelem Vitte, 1923), I, n. 46. Hereafter cited as *De virtute Obedientiae.*

[6] D. (1. 2) 2. 1, 14.

[7] D. (1. 2) 2. 16.

[8] D. (1. 2) 2, 17–19, 27. Cf. M. Van de Kerckhove, "De notione jurisdictionis in jure romano"—*Jus Pontificium,* XVI (1936), 49–65. Hereafter *Jus Pontificium* will be cited as *JP.*

[9] N. (131.3); N. (120.6). "Itaque iurisdictio facta est synonimia vocabuli 'potestatis,' non sensu romano classico, sed potestatis in genere, vocabulum proinde omnino genericum et qua tale omnibus ramis ordinis administrativi applicabilis."—M. Van de Kerckhove, "De notione jurisdictionis in iure romano"—*JP,* XVI (1936), 62.

meaning of the term *jurisdiction* as found in the Novels of Justinian was taken into the terminology of the Church at the time of Gregory the Great (590–604), although it was not frequently used during the following five centuries, and occurs only rarely in the *Decretum Gratiani.*[10] Instead, expressions such as *ditio,*[11] *auctoritas*[12] and *curam animarum habere*[13] are found, which expressions in their meaning point to a general administrative power.[14]

In the thirteenth century the term *jurisdiction* was restricted in its conceptual scope. At the beginning of the thirteenth century the term pointed, as it had done since the time of Gregory the Great, to the general administration of spiritual and temporal matters. But Huguccio (+ 1210) limited the comprehension of the term by excluding the administration of temporal matters from its scope. With this distinction the term *jurisdiction* referred only to power in the spiritual sphere, to acts depending on the power of orders.[15] From that time to the present, jurisdiction has signified the public power of a perfect society.[16]

The practice of referring to the authority of the Church in the internal forum with the use of the term jurisdiction began in the thirteenth century.[17] The *potestas ligandi et solvendi* had always been attributed to the sacerdotal order, and hence was not identified with jurisdiction. Joannes Teutonicus (+ 1245) in his *Summa ad Decretum,* knowing the opinion of the canonists on this point, only with some timidity admitted that the *key* was *jurisdiction.*[18] However, in 1234 Saint Raymond of Pennafort

[10] Cf. c. 39, C. XI, q. I; c. 52, C. XVI, q. 1.

[11] C. 34, C. XXIV, q. I.

[12] C. 10, D. XCVI.

[13] C. 6, C. XVI, q. II.

[14] Cf. M. Van de Kerckhove, "De notione jurisdictionis in jure romano" —*JP,* XVI (1936), 63–65.

[15] *Summa,* glossa ad c. X, q. 1., introd., Cod. Vat. Lat. 2280, fol. 163 r . . . as cited by M. Van de Kerckhove, "De notione jurisdictionis apud Decretistas et Priores Decretalistas"—*JP,* XVIII (1938), 12.

[16] M. Van de Kerckhove, "De notione jurisdictionis apud Decretistas et Priores Decretalistas"—*JP,* XVIII (1938), 11.

[17] M. Van de Kerckhove, "De notione jurisdictionis apud Decretistas et Priores Decretalistas"—*JP,* XVIII (1938), 13.

[18] *Summa ad decretum,* glossa Palatina ad dist. XX, c. 1., Claves, Cod.

(1175–1275) had confirmed this opinion, and admitted even then that others also held the key to be jurisdiction.[19]

Thus it was at the middle of the thirteenth century that canonists called jurisdiction the public power of ruling a perfect community. Jurisdiction was distinguished as either of the external or of the internal forum, but the distinction between the sacramental and extra-sacramental aspects of the internal forum had not yet been made. From the time of the thirteenth century the word jurisdiction has retained with canonists its meaning of the public power of ruling a perfect society.[20]

2. *Present Meaning*

In canon 196 the Code designates the source of the power of jurisdiction, and enumerates the divisions according to the forums. It does not define terms but rather makes *iurisdictio* and *regimen* synonymous notions.[21] Nevertheless the use of the word *regimen* implies that the definition of jurisdiction has not changed from the thirteenth century, and that the Code understands jurisdiction as ruling power, that is, as the power of ruling a perfect society with legislative, judicial and coercive authority.[22]

More precisely, jurisdiction may be defined as *the public power, granted to a legitimate Superior by Christ or the Church through a canonical mission, of directing and ruling the baptized to eternal*

Vat. 658, fol. 5 r ". . . sed credo clavem iurisdictionem esse," as cited by M. Van de Kerckhove, "De notione iurisdicitionis apud Decretistas et Priores Decretalistas"—*JP,* XVIII (1938), 14.

19 ". . . alii autem dicunt, et credo verius, quod nonnisi una sit clavis, quae quidem est potestas seu iurisdictio." *Summa de casibus* (ed. nova, Veronae, 1744), lib. III, tit. XXIV, § 5, pp. 451–452.

20 "Ad conclusionem generalem sic pervenimus, quod in doctrina canonistarum inde ab anno 1210 usque ad annum 1250 iam praeformatam habemus disciplinam can. 196. Ipsae autem voces 'fori interni sacramentalis sive extra-sacramentalis' nondum apparent."—M. Van de Kerckhove, "De notione jurisdictionis apud Decretistas et Priores Decretalistas"—JP, XVIII (1938), 14.

21 "Potestas iurisdictionis seu regiminis quae ex divina institutione est in Ecclesia, alia est fori externi, alia fori interni, seu conscientiae, sive sacramentalis sive extra-sacramentalis."

22 Chelodi, *Ius de Personis,* n. 125.

life.[23] It is called a *public power* to mark it off from dominative power, which is a private power and is found in imperfect societies like religious institutes. It is granted *by Christ* to the Roman Pontiff on the occasion of his valid election and acceptance thereof. From that moment the Pope possesses supreme and full jurisdiction over the entire Church in matters which pertain to faith, morals and discipline.[24] Jurisdiction is also granted *by the Church through a canonical mission.* It is from this mission that a Bishop receives jurisdiction on taking canonical possession of his diocese,[25] and Superiors in clerical exempt religious institutes according to the norm of the particular Constitutions and the common law.[26]

By the addition to the definition of the phrase *"ruling the baptized to eternal life,"* jurisdiction is clearly distinguished from the power of orders, which is intended directly and proximately for the promotion of divine worship and the sanctification of souls. Ruling power contains in itself all jurisdictional power, legislative, judicial, coercive; for the power of jurisdiction and the power of ruling denote the same concept in canon law.[27] The *baptized* are the subjects over whom the ruling power of the Church is exercised. Those who have received valid baptism are the individuals who are to be directed and led by the Church to eternal life.[28]

3. *Division*

Jurisdiction according to the *forum* is divided into that of the *external* and that of the *internal* forum.[29] The reason for this division is found in the fact that the Church is a society different from the State, which is also a perfect society. The Church is a spiritual and supernatural society established to promote its own social end and to obtain the sanctification of souls. Consequently

---

[23] Vermeersch-Creusen, *Epitome Iuris Canonici cum Commentariis ad Scholas et ad Usum Privatum* (3 vols., Vol. I, 3. ed., Mechliniae-Romae: Dessain, 1937), I, n. 312. Hereafter cited as *Epitome*.

[24] Canons 218, § 1; 219.

[25] Canon 334, § 2.

[26] Canon 501, § 1.

[27] Canon 196: "Potestas iurisdictionis seu regiminis. . . ."

[28] Canon 87.

[29] Canon 196.

the Church directs and rules not only the supernatural society in general, and the members of it taken as a group; it also directly and immediately plans for the eternal salvation of each individual.[30]

Jurisdiction is of the *external forum* inasmuch as the good of the community is primarily and directly intended in its use. It is concerned with the social actions of the individual, the actions which have a relation to the Church as well as to God, and the actions which are placed before the Church to be judged as good or bad.[31]

Jurisdiction of the *internal forum* is exercised directly and primarily for the good of the individual members of the Church, though indirectly and secondarily the social good of the Church is also promoted through the progress of the members. In this instance the Church considers the conscience and the good of an individual inasmuch as he is a private person, and not in his relation to others as a member of the social group.[32] Thus the confessor with the necessary jurisdictional faculties in the *internal forum* uses these faculties in the sacrament of penance to advance the spiritual condition of the baptized subject. Nevertheless, the grant of jurisdiction by the Ordinary to confessors is an act which primarily concerns the good of the Church as a social institution, and therefore is regarded as belonging to the *external* forum.[33]

By reason of the title through which it is entrusted to a subject, jurisdiction may be *ordinary* or *delegated.* If it is attached by law to an office, it is called *ordinary* jurisdiction. If it is granted to a person, it is called *delegated* jurisdiction. Ordinary jurisdiction is *proper* when inherent by law in an office and when exercised in the incumbent's own name and not in the name of another. When by law jurisdiction is attached to an office to be

---

30 Maroto, *Institutiones Iuris Canonici ad Normam Novi Codicis* (2 vols., Vol. I, Matriti, 1919), I, n. 718. Hereafter cited as *Institutiones.*

31 Vermeersch-Creusen, *Epitome,* I, n. 313; Chelodi, *Ius de Personis,* n. 125.

32 Vermeersch-Creusen, *Epitome,* I. n. 313; Chelodi, *Ius de Personis,* n. 125.

33 Maroto, *Institutiones,* I, n. 722.

exercised in the name of another, it is called *vicarious ordinary* jurisdiction.[34]

Jurisdiction is either *contentious* or *voluntary* inasmuch as it is exercised in judicial or non-judicial matters.[35]

Territorial jurisdiction is that which extends over a certain place or territory, while *personal* jurisdiction is that which encompasses those who are subject to it, even apart from any consideration of the territory in which they are located.

C. DOMINATIVE POWER

Corresponding to the power of jurisdiction in the Church, a perfect society, there exists a dominative power exercised in a religious institute, an imperfect society. By means of this power the superior of the imperfect society is able to direct the actions of its members to the fulfillment of the aims of the society.

Dominative power may arise from the law of nature, as in the case of a father over his family, or from a contract or agreement, as in the case of professed religious who by their religious profession place themselves under the authority of the superiors, or finally, by the law of nature together with a contract, as happens in marriage when the wife is under the power of her husband.[36]

Dominative power is proper to an imperfect society. Its nature will depend upon the nature of the society in which it is exercised. It is called " dominative " for the reason that superiors endowed with this power have, as it were, a certain dominion over their subjects.[37]

Blat [38] traces the development of dominative power from an original condition of master and slave to the later condition of "*societas herilis*," in which a free contract was made between master and servant. This power of master over servant was a private power. It was given the name of dominative power.

[34] Canon 197, §§ 1, 2. Maroto, *Institutiones*, I, n. 697.

[35] Canon 201, §§ 2, 3.

[36] Raus, *De Virtute Obedientiae*, I, n. 41.

[37] Raus, *De Virtute Obedientiae*, I, n. 41.

[38] " De Potestate Superiorum in Religionibus secundum Codicem I. C."—*Commentarium pro Religiosis et Missionariis*, XVI (1935), 324. Hereafter cited as *CpRM*.

Dominative power as existing in a religious society is a private power. It takes its origin from the contract made at religious profession, by which a religious subjects himself to a Superior and promises to obey according to the purpose of the society. The power possessed by the Superiors is not unlimited or arbitrary. It depends upon the end of the religious institute, and also on the regulations imposed by the perfect society, the Church.[39]

The Code makes mention of dominative power in canons 501, § 1,[40] and 1312, § 1,[41] without, however, giving a definition of the term. Clancy[42] in his definition of dominative power includes all the requisite elements. He defines it as "that authority which a superior has over his subjects in virtue of their enrollment in the community, and by reason of which he governs their actions, within limits defined by the Code of Canon Law and the particular Constitutions of the institute, to the attainment of the end or purpose of the society."

D. DISTINCTION BETWEEN JURISDICTION AND DOMINATIVE POWER

Perfect societies arise from the law of nature and possess the public power of ruling the community. The extent of the power invested in the Superiors depends on the nature of the society.

Religious institutes, as imperfect societies, arise by reason of the permission and approval of the Church,[43] a perfect society, and possess a private power to direct the religious to the fulfillment of the purpose of the institute. The extent of the authority follows from the nature of these societies and the limits placed

---

[39] Raus, *De Virtute Obedientiae,* I, n. 41.

[40] Superiores et Capitula, ad normam constitutionum et iuris communis, potestatem habent dominativam in subditos; in religione autem clericali exempta, habent iurisdictionem ecclesiasticam tam pro foro interno, quam pro externo.

[41] Qui potestatem dominativam in voluntatem voventis legitime exercet, potest eius vota valide et, ex iusta causa, etiam licite irrita reddere, ita ut nullo in casu obligatio postea reviviscat.

[42] *The Local Religious Superior,* The Catholic University of America Canon Law Studies, n. 175 (Washington, D. C.: The Catholic University of America Press, 1943), p. 8.

[43] Canon 492, § 1.

on them by the Church. Hence, in perfect societies there is jurisdiction or public power; in imperfect societies, private power. The authority in each depends on the nature and purpose of the society. The imperfect society has the further restriction of being limited by all the laws of the perfect society of which it is a component element.

In some religious institutes the Superiors possess not only the power which is proper to an imperfect society, but share also in the ruling power of the Church, the perfect society. They acquire both jurisdiction and dominative power.[44] It is clear that the Superior is using the power of jurisdiction when he grants faculties to his priests to hear the confession of his own religious subjects,[45] to preach to them,[46] and to dispense the religious from the ecclesiastical precept of fast and abstinence.[47] It is also clear that in the ordinary affairs of everyday community life the Superiors are exercising dominative power, as when they grant the usual permissions according to the Constitutions, and dispense from the acts of the community observance. But in cases of doubt whether jurisdiction or dominative power is being used, it seems that the decision rests in discovering whether the particular act of the Superior primarily tends to the fulfillment of the purpose of the Church or of the religious institute. If the act tends primarily to the former, it is an act of jurisdiction; if to the latter, it is an act of dominative power.[48]

[44] Canon 501, § 1.
[45] Canon 875, § 1.
[46] Canon 1338, § 1.
[47] Canon 1245, § 3.
[48] Cf. Clancy, *The Local Religious Superior,* pp. 10, 11.

PART I

HISTORICAL SYNOPSIS

CHAPTER II

THE SPIRITUAL CARE OF THE RELIGIOUS PRIOR TO THE IV GENERAL COUNCIL OF THE LATERAN

ARTICLE I. VESTIGES OF THE INSTITUTE OF SPIRITUAL PREFECT IN THE MONASTIC RULES OF THE EAST

A. HERMITS OF SAINT ANTHONY

The monks of Saint Anthony (251–356) in the Egyptian desert received their fundamental training from Saint Anthony himself. Those wishing to become religious hermits went to this man, the founder of monasticism, and were guided by him until they were sufficiently grounded in the principles of the religious life to take up their abode far from the nearest hermit.[1]

With the completion of the primary training every man was left very much to himself according to his own discretion. The monks visited one another from time to time to discourse on spiritual subjects, and the elders, because of their knowledge of the religious life and their experience, exerted a *personal* influence on the young. Corrections were offered and rebukes were occasionally given by the fellow monks. But there was no individual, officially so designated, to give conferences and exhortations to the monks. Any hermit who chose an instructor and director made this decision voluntarily.[2] These early hermits of Saint Anthony were not clerics.[3]

B. RULE OF SAINT PACHOMIUS

The Rule of Saint Pachomius (ca. 292–346) required spiritual instruction to be given at three different periods: (a) before

[1] Butler, *Lausiac History of Palladius* (Cambridge, 1898), pp. 230–234.

[2] Butler, *Benedictine Monachism* (1. ed., London: Longmans Green and Co., 1919), p. 12. Hereafter cited as *Benedictine Monachism.*

[3] Butler, *Benedictine Monachism,* pp. 14, 15.

admission to the monastery;[4] (b) during the period of training;[5] and (c) after official admission into the community.[6]

In the first period the rudiments of the monastic life were taught; in the second period a more complete instruction was presented; in the final period selected subject matter concerning religious perfection and discipline was treated two or three times each week by the Superior. The importance attached to these conferences given by the Superior can be judged by the fact that a most grave cause was necessary to permit a monk to be licitly absent from them. Thus at the time of Saint Pachomius there existed beyond a doubt a regulation requiring public instruction to be given by the Superior of the monks. It is also worthy of note that an assistant was appointed to aid the Superior, probably in this particular share of his office.[7]

C. Rule of Saint Basil

The ancient Rule of Saint Basil (330–379) was not very specific concerning the conferences and the person to whom the obligation of imparting instruction was entrusted. The Superior was the leader of his brethren in the entire community life,[8] and most likely the duty of teaching and instructing the brethren fell to him. The Superior was given an assistant, who was expected to supervise the needs of the community when the Superior was absent. One of the duties of the assistant consisted in encouraging those individuals who were inclined to dejection and sadness.[9]

Article II. Vestiges of the Institute of Spiritual Prefect in the Monastic Rules of the West

A. Rule of Cassian

The Rule written by Cassian (ca. 360–435) for his monastery

[4] *Regula S. Pachomii*—Migne, *Patrologiae Cursus Completus, Series Latina* (221 vols., Parisiis, 1844–1855), XXIII, 70, 78. Hereafter cited as *MPL.*

[5] *Regula S. Pachomii—MPL,* XXIII, 78.

[6] *Regula S. Pachomii—MPL,* XXIII, 67, 80, 85.

[7] *Regula S. Pachomii—MPL,* XXIII, 83, 84.

[8] *Regulae Fusius Tractatae*—Migne, *Patrologiae Cursus Completus, Series Graeca* (161 vols., Parisiis, 1857–1866), XXXI, 987. Hereafter cited as *MPG.*

[9] *Regulae Fusius Tractatae—MPG,* XXXI, 1031.

in France, like the Rule of Saint Pachomius, enumerated three stages in the spiritual instruction of the man desiring to be a monk. These stages included the time before admission to the monastery, the period of training and the years following official reception into the community.[10]

The Rule did not name any authority in the monastery to whom the spiritual instruction was entrusted as a duty. Cassian, the author of the Rule, having lived in the East in his early years and observed the eastern hermits, was influenced by the example of Saint Anthony, who advocated that those who sought the higher life should learn from the religious already in possession of the desired virtues. Consequently the direction for the members of the community came not from a master appointed by law, but from the companion singled out by the individual monk. It was a relationship of teacher and disciple, not superior and subject; it was voluntary and not imposed by rule.

B. RULE OF SAINT AUGUSTINE

Saint Augustine (354–430), in two sermons treating of his religious community in Africa and in a letter written to a group of religious women, gave norms which influenced the founders of later religious societies, notably Saint Norbert (ca. 1080–1134). The letter written to the religious women is almost exclusively of an instructive and exhortatory character, containing general invitations, encouraging the practice of virtue rather than strict rules commanding specific duties, as is the practice in the composition of the present-day rules of religious institutes.

However, it is clear that according to the desire of Saint Augustine the Superior was to be obeyed as a father. To him fell the duty of giving instructions, admonitions and exhortations. He had to correct any faults he saw in the religious. Fraternal correction of one another was also desired of the members of the society as supplementary to the direction given by the Superior.[11]

C. RULE OF SAINT BENEDICT

It was taken for granted in the early Benedictine family that

[10] *De Coenobiorum Institutis—MPL,* XLIX, 150, 154, 158–164.

[11] *Regula ad Servos Dei, MPL,* XXXII, 1384.

the ordinary applicant for admission would not be a candidate for the priesthood. If he was a priest, or a lesser cleric, he received no special privilege by reason of his dignity. The subject was a religious, either lay or clerical. It is an historical fact that in the early days most of the members were lay; yet clerics were not forbidden admission.[12]

By the profession of vows a man became a juridical member of the Benedictine family under the power of the Abbot, the father of the family. The Abbot nurtured and supervised the development of the young monk's spiritual life. He followed the apostolic form "Reprove—Entreat—Rebuke." He reproved the restless and undisciplined; he entreated and implored and encouraged the obedient, the meek, the patient; he rebuked the negligent. He was not to connive at sin in its beginnings, but to pluck it out by the roots. He was to correct the upright and intelligent verbally for the first and second transgressions, but was to administer and apply physical chastisement to the disobedient and stubborn and proud.[13]

If the monastic family became too large for immediate supervision and vigilance by the Abbot, he chose religious of good reputation and holy manner of life as assistants in the government of the monastery. These assistants were called Deans. They exercised as much authority as was delegated to them by the Abbot. They were selected on account of their virtuous lives and their prudence in ruling others. Length of time in the monastic family was not one of the requirements for the appointment.[14]

The Abbot, then, was the father who had the obligation of leading the members of his family to their heavenly home. He had to correct and admonish the community as a whole, as well as the individuals within the community. If the family became too large for his paternal guidance, he appointed assistants and delegated sufficient authority to them.

At the time of Saint Benedict (480–543) there was no indica-

---

[12] Butler, *Sancti Benedicti Regula Monasteriorum, Editio Critico-Practica* (2 ed., Friburgi Brisgoviae: Herder, 1927), cap. LXII. Hereafter cited as *Regula Sancti Benedicti.*

[13] Butler, *Regula Sancti Benedicti,* cap. II.

[14] Butler, *Regula Sancti Benedicti,* cap. XXI.

tion that ecclesiastical jurisdiction was exercised by the Abbot. It is later in history that the period of exemption began. Nevertheless it is clear from the constitution of the monastic family and from the profession of vows that the Superior possessed dominative power.

Article III. From Saint Benedict to the IV General Council of the Lateran

From the time of St. Benedict to the IV General Council of the Lateran (1215), the legislation given by the Popes to religious institutes contained scanty material dealing with the internal rule of a religious community. As the Church expanded and the faith took root among new peoples, monasteries sprang up everywhere, and the Rule of St. Benedict, carried by the missionaries, formed the basis for the new communities. This Rule designated the superiors and determined the method they should employ in guiding the religious family. As a consequence, additional and more complete legislation by the Popes and Councils was not thought necessary for regulating the internal rule of a monastery except when abuses arose or circumstances changed the original constitution of the monastery.

But while papal legislation concerning discipline within the monastery was very meager, nevertheless hundreds of papal documents attest the fact that the Popes constantly wrote to these monasteries concerning their juridic relations with the bishops. From the time of Pope Gregory I (590–604) to that of Innocent III (1198–1216) innumerable rights and privileges were bestowed upon the monasteries by the successive Popes. The content of these letters concerned chiefly the exemption of the monasteries from the jurisdiction of the bishops, the juridic relations between bishops and the monasteries, and the election of the Abbot. From these documents two facts stand out: (a) the concession, confirmation and extension of the privilege of exemption, and (b) the concession of jurisdiction to the Abbot with the power to delegate his authority to others. Since in the fourteenth century the priest appointed to supervise the training of the students in religious institutes possessed jurisdiction as well as dominative power, it is appropriate to consider briefly both these historical privileges, namely, the removal of the monasteries from the authority of the Bishops, and the concession of jurisdiction to the Superiors of the monasteries.

A. PERIOD OF GENERAL EXEMPTION

With the growth of monasticism in the West the older established monasteries constituted new filial houses which were subject to the parent house in matters of discipline. In the days before exemptions were granted, uniformity and discipline among the houses were difficult to observe because each monastery received particular statutes from the Bishop of the territory. In order to preserve a common discipline, a group of abbots in the monasteries of Africa offered a plan to the Bishop of Africa whereby the religious would be exempted from all the Bishops except one, the Primate of Africa. This privilege was granted to them in the Synod of Africa held about 525.[15]

Gregory I (590–604), a Benedictine monk, granted partial exemption to a monastery in Ravenna.[16] But it was the monastery of Bobbio that obtained from Pope Honorius I (625–638) what was probably the first grant of total exemption from episcopal power.[17] Later in the same century Pope Adeodatus II (672–676) bestowed the privilege of exemption on the monastery of St. Martin of Tours,[18] and the monastery of Farfa in 817 received

---

[15] Mansi, *Sacrorum Conciliorum Nova et Amplissima Collectio* (53 vols. in 60, Paris, Leipzig, Arnhem, 1901–1927), VIII, 635–650. Hereafter cited as Mansi. Harduinus, *Acta Conciliorum et Epistolae Decretales ac Constitutiones Summorum Pontificum* (ed. Regia, 12 vols., 1715).

[16] Epist. "*Quam sit necessarium,*" apr. 598—Jaffé, *Regesta Pontificum Romanorum* (2. ed., correctam et auctam auspiciis Gulielmi Wattenbach curaverunt S. Loewenfeld, F. Kaltenbrunner, P. Ewald, 2 vols. in 1, Lipsiae, 1885–1888), 1504. Hereafter the letter J will be joined with the letters L, K or E, to designate the editors.

[17] Epist. "*Si semper,*" 11 ian. 628—JE; *Bullarum Diplomatum et Privilegiorum Sanctorum Romanorum Pontificum Taurinensis Editio* (25 vols., Augustae Taurinorum, 1857–1872), I, 169. Hereafter cited as *Bull. Rom. Taur.* Cf. Montalembert, *Monks of the West* (2 vols., Boston, 1872), I, 397, 398.

[18] Epist. "*Aequitatis nos admonet,*" date uncertain, but between 672–676—JE, n. 2105; Mansi, XI, 103; *Bull. Rom. Taur.*, I. 208.

a similar grant from Pope Stephen IV (816–817).[19] Pope Gregory IV (828–844), in a letter to the bishops and people of France, granted jurisdiction to the Abbot of Fleury. In order that any ecclesiastic or dignitary might ordain or even say mass at the abbey, the permission of the Abbot was required.[20]

From the ninth century papal documents abound with their exemption privileges granted to the monasteries in Italy, France and Germany. The *Bullarium Romanum* contains innumerable documents exempting the monasteries from the jurisdiction of the bishop, and others signifying approbation of these grants by succeeding popes together with additional concessions. These concessions were continued to the time of the IV General Council of the Lateran. The importance of these privileges as regards the present study is that the power of jurisdiction was conferred in order to be exercised in the monastery. The next obvious step is the consideration of the subject of this power, that is, the office in which the power of jurisdiction was vested.

B. JURISDICTION AND DOMINATIVE POWER IN THE ABBOT

In the letters of the Popes granting exemptions to the monasteries the Abbot was named as the one upon whom jurisdiction was bestowed. The amount of jurisdiction granted to a monastery depended on the extent to which the monastery was exempted from the authority of the Bishop. But when the jurisdiction was given, if the monastery was ruled by an Abbot, it was the Abbot always who was the recipient. Thus at Fleury Bishops could not ordain, Bishops and priests could not say mass, without the permission of the Abbot.[21] The same was true at the monasteries of Fulda [22] and Corbie.[23]

---

[19] Epist., "*Cum magna nobis,*" 23 ian. 817—JE, n. 2544; *Bull. Rom. Taur.*, I, 262; *MPL*, CXXIX, 973.

[20] Epist. "*Quoniam ex Apostolica,*" apr. 829—JE, n. 2570; *Bull. Rom. Taur.*, I, 280; *MPL*, CXXIX, 995.

[21] Gregorius IV (828–844), epist. "*Quoniam ex Apostolica,*" apr. 829—JE, n. 2570; *Bull. Rom. Taur.*, I, 280; *MPL*, CXXIX, 995.

[22] Zacharias (741–752), epist. "*Quoniam semper,*" 4 nov. 751—JE, n. 2663; *Bull. Rom. Taur.*, I, 238; *MPL*, LXXXIX, 954; Mansi, XII, 349.

[23] Benedictus III (855–858), epist. "*Cum Romanae Sedis,*" 7 oct. 855—JE, n. 2293; *Bull. Rom. Taur.*, I, 295; *MPL*, CXV, 693.

It was the decision of Pope John XI (931–936) that the Abbot of Cluny could receive under his jurisdiction any monks who desired to strive for greater perfection.[24] The powers of the Abbot were increased constantly, so that he came to exercise jurisdiction over spiritual and temporal matters. But it was always to the Abbot, if the monastery was ruled by an Abbot, to whom the jurisdiction was entrusted, and not to any other official in the monastery. If a monastery did not have an Abbot, then this power was vested in the conventual Prior. These men at the head of the monastic family possessed both jurisdictional and dominative power.

Several instances are found in papal letters in which the Popes, because of a dispute in the monastery, either explicitly emphasized the power of the Abbot or more clearly defined the extent of the Superior's power. Thus Pope Pelagius I (555–560) wrote to a certain Opilionus and stated that the monks had no power to depose an Abbot. He gave as a reason the accepted fact that all power in the monastery was vested in the Abbot, and not in any of the religious subjects.[25] Likewise John VI (701–705) in 704, after granting certain privileges to a monastery at Brescia, exhorted the religious to obey their Abbot, *Praepositus* and Prior.[26]

The term "prior" occurred frequently in the Rule of St. Benedict, but it was applied indiscriminately to all those acting as Superiors, be they Abbots, *Praepositi* or Deans. The *Praepositus* in the Rule of St. Benedict was the first assistant to the Abbot.[27] This office was later supplanted in a gradual manner by the office of the Prior. In the eighth century the terms *Praepositus* and Prior signified those officials who acted as assistant to the Abbot and possessed the degree of authority given them by the Abbot. In the ninth and tenth centuries the term Prior acquired a very specific meaning. It was used to designate either the Superior in

---

[24] Epist. "*Convenit apostolico moderamini,*" mart. 931—JL, n. 3584; *MPL,* CXXXII, 1055.

[25] Epist. "*Nullam potestatem,*"—JE, n. 1001; Mansi, 910.

[26] Epist. "*Salubre nimis est,*"—*Bull. Rom. Taur.,* I, 213–215.

[27] Butler, *Regula Sancti Benedicti,* cap. LXV; *Benedictine Monachism,* pp. 216 seqq.

a monastery without an Abbot, or the first assistant in a monastery which had an Abbot. In the first case he was called the conventual Prior, and usually had all the authority ordinarily possessed by the Abbot. In the second instance he was given the title of claustral Prior, and exercised that amount of power which was delegated to him by the Abbot.

Urban III (1185–1187), wishing to correct abuses and to settle disputes in the monastery of Grandmont, wrote to the prior and monks to affirm clearly the authority of the prior. The latter had full power in spiritual and temporary matters. No one else could exercise jurisdiction without receiving delegated jurisdiction from the prior. Concerning the *spiritual care of the clerics* the pope emphasized that the Prior or his delegate were the only ones possessing the authority to make corrections and impose penances. No other person in the monastery could usurp this power.[28]

Honorius III (1216–1227) wrote to the same monastery, reiterated the rules of his predecessor and added more detailed regulations. The pontiff stated that a priest, delegated by the prior, and having full power over a determined number of clerics and lay brothers, should be designated for the spiritual care of these religious. To this priest was granted the authority to make corrections and to rebuke the monks for their disobedient actions. To exercise the office of correcting, the priest assembled the monks at stated intervals, read a passage from the Constitutions or some other book helpful to progress in the spiritual life, and thereupon offered an explanation of the reading. Sometimes instructions alone were given, but if there was need to make a correction, it was done after the delegated priest had given his explanation of the reading.[29]

Innocent III (1198–1216) wrote to the convent and Abbot of Subiaco, instructing the monks on the manner of conducting themselves in community life, and giving norms to the superiors

---

[28] *Epist. "Quanto per infusionem,"* 15 iulii 1186—*Bull. Rom. Taur.*, III, 43, 44; *MPL*, CCII, 1416.

[29] Epist. *"Ad sopiendam materiam,"* 1 mart. 1219—*Bull. Rom. Taur.*, III, 351–355; Potthast, *Regesta Pontificum Romanorum inde ab anno post Christum natum MCXCVIII ad annum MCCCIV* (2 vols., Berolini, 1874–1875), n. 5998.

to increase the efficacy and fruitfulness of the rule. The Abbot was required to exercise a vigilant care and diligent solicitude in regard to each member in the community. He was required to correct and instruct the monks and work unceasingly for their spiritual advancement. If he proved negligent in these duties, he was held responsible for the offenses of his religious.[30] The Pope also marked out the duties of the claustral prior. The office of the latter consisted in instructing the monks by word and example, in correcting and reproving offenses, and in encouraging the zealous to strive for greater perfection.[31]

[30] C. 6, X, *de statu monachorum,* III, 35; *MPL,* CCXIV, 1064.
[31] *Loc. cit.*

CHAPTER III

FROM THE TIME OF THE IV GENERAL COUNCIL OF THE LATERAN TO THE CODE

ARTICLE I. REGULATIONS FOR THE CISTERCIANS AND THE BLACK MONKS OF SAINT BENEDICT

At the beginning of the thirteenth century a new type of religious institute, the Mendicants, made its appearance. Instead of communities each one legally separate from the others, the Mendicants founded monasteries juridically dependent on one another and subject to a central superior. In each house of the order there were established a conventual prior and his assistant. Authority was vested in the prior, and the assistant received only that amount of power which was granted to him by the prior or by the Rule.

During this time the abbeys continued to exist under the older Rules with no change in their Constitutions as regards the Superiors and the government of the abbeys. However, in 1311 Pope Clement V (1305–1314) added several canons to those of the Council of Vienne (1311–1312), one of which concerned the internal rule of the monasteries. The Pope ordered that in the Benedictine monasteries the Rule should be explained to the younger members by an instructor appointed by the proper authority. Likewise a competent teacher should be given to the novices for the purpose of instructing them in the divine office as well as in the observance of the community exercises.[1]

In the same century Pope Benedict XII (1334–1342) enacted regulations for the Cistercians and the Black Monks of St. Benedict in order that the spiritual life of their students might progress harmoniously with their intellectual activity. In the Constitution *Fulgens sicut stella*[2] he issued the norms for the reformation of

[1] C. I, *de statu monachorum vel canonicorum regularium,* III, 10, in Clem.

[2] 12 iul. 1335—*Bull. Rom. Taur.,* IV. 343.

the Cistercian Order. The Pontiff, among other matters, commanded the Abbots to appoint *Rectors* for students engaged in studies outside the monastery. The *Rectors* of the students had full authority over them. They were given charge of the souls entrusted to them, and were authorized to correct and absolve them in the same manner as the Abbot. The students, nevertheless, remained subject also to their Abbot.[3]

In the following year the same Pope ordered a similar procedure to be observed by the Black Monks of St. Benedict. In order to insure the observance of the regular discipline when the students were absent from the monastery for the purpose of studies, the Abbot or Prior nearest to the house of studies was required to appoint for one year a priest to act as the *Prior of the students.* He had full authority to correct, punish, absolve, dispense, just as the Abbot in the respective home monastery of each religious. *The Prior of the students* was to instruct, to teach, to mould the students according to the norms of the monastic discipline. He was to lead them both by word and example. Finally he made a report to the respective monasteries on the student's return at the completion of studies.[4]

Article II. The Constitution " Cum ad regularem "

The Council of Trent (1545–1563) enacted many decrees and canons for the reformation of Regulars in general, but very few which pertained to the education and spiritual training of the novices and the professed clerical students. Clement VIII (1592–1605), intending to supplement the decrees and canons of the Council, the legislation of the Popes and the rules of the various religious orders, promulgated the Constitution *Cum ad regularem* on March 19, 1603. This decree was concerned chiefly with the

[3] "Et ut eisdem studentibus animarum cura non desit, volumus et ordinamus, quod in eisdem Studiis generalibus abbates ipsorum Studiorum rectores deputent idoneos provisores, qui curam habeant animarum studentium in eisdem, quique illos corrigant et absolvant, sicut proprii abbates subditos proprie corrigere et absolvere possunt in monasteriis eorumdem; propter hoc tamen dicti studentes a potestate proprii abbatis exempti aliquatenus non existant."—*Bull. Rom. Taur.*, IV, 343.

[4] Benedictus XII, const. "Summi Magistri," 20 iun. 1336—*Bull. Rom. Taur.*, IV, 359–360.

training and education of the novices, and the qualities and duties of the Master of novices. So thorough and concise was its treatment of these subjects that subsequent papal legislation has scarcely added or revoked any points in the clearly stated law of Clement VIII. It was in this papal document that the same Pope constituted an office in monasteries of Regulars to provide for the spiritual training of the young clerics.[5]

Pope Benedict XII (1334–1342) had required that a priest be appointed to provide for the spiritual care of the clerical students of the Cistercians and the Black Monks of St. Benedict while these were engaged in studies outside their respective monasteries. Pope Clement VIII (1592–1605) went further. He demanded that priests be appointed in monasteries of Regulars to provide for the spiritual training of clerical students even though the students did not leave the monastery for their studies. The constitution which enacted this rule was directed by Pope Clement VIII to Italy and the adjacent islands.[6] It seems that this Constitution of its own force never imposed an obligation on Regulars beyond the limits of the territory for which the legislation was originally enacted.

But in 1624 the Sacred Congregation of the Council renewed and confirmed the *general decrees* of Clement VIII which concerned the reformation of Regulars and the reception, profession and training of the novices.[7] However, the Constitution *Cum*

[5] Clemens VIII, const. "*Cum ad regularem,*" 19 mart. 1603, § 20—*Codicis Iuris Canonici Fontes cura Emi Petri Gasparri editi* (9 vols.), Romae (postea Civitate Vaticana): Typis Polyglottis Vaticanis (1923–1939), (Vols. VII, VIII, IX, ed. cura et studio Emi Iustiniani Card. Serédi), n. 189; hereafter cited as *Fontes.*

[6] Bachofen, *Compendium Iuris Regularium* (New York, 1903), p. 74; Wernz, *Ius Decretalium* (6 vols., Romae et Prati, 1898–1905), III, 376, n. (262).

[7] ". . . ac primo, ut infecta semina, e quibus pravi eiusmodi fructus potissimum prodeunt, deinceps ne serantur in vinea Domini, censuit, esse innovandas, et Sanctissimi authoritate innovat Constitutiones, et Decreta *generalia* sanct. mem. Clementis VIII ad Regularium reformationem, ac Novitiorum receptionem, professionem, atque institutionem spectantia, districteque praecepit Generalibus, atque aliis omnibus Ordinum Superioribus ut illa exacte observent, atque, ut observentur, efficiant, sub poenis statutis in iisdem Constitutionibus."—*Fontes,* n. 2454. Italics inserted in the text by the writer.

ad regularem contained *particular* and not *general* decrees, and though it appears that the Sacred Congregation of the Council had this Constitution in mind inasmuch as it explicitly mentioned the novitiate, yet a doubt has always remained among the authors.[8]

Pope Clement VIII explained the duty of the priest charged with the care of the students by showing the relation of his duty with that which is placed on another priest in the novitiate. During the year of probation the aspirant to religious profession is given a fundamental training by the Master of novices in the discipline of the community. One year, however, is not sufficient for the ordinary novice to become firmly established in the practice of virtue. In order to make solid and secure what is begun and acquired in the novitiate, the young clerical professed religious must be placed under the direction of a Superior, who will strive, during the years the students prepare for the priesthood, to perfect the work begun by the Master of novices.[9] This office of the Superior was the one constituted by Clement VIII for Regulars. The priest assigned to the work exercised an office in relation to the clerical professed students similar to that exercised by the Master over the novices. He was not given any title in the decree of Clement VIII except for the fact that he was called a Superior.[10]

The *place* in which the students were to live during the days of preparation for the priesthood could be either the novitiate house or some other monastery which did not serve as a novitiate. If the students remained in the novitiate, they occupied a place

[8] Wernz, *Ius Decretalium,* III, 376, n. (262): "Neque quidquam probat decreta Clementis VIII 25 Jun. 1599 et 19 Mar. 1603 . . . postea publicata esse generalia; etenim demonstrari nequit in generalibus decretis hanc specialem ordinationem esse extensam." Cf. Vermeersch, *De Religiosis Institutis et Personis* (2 vols., Brugis, Romae et Ratisbonae, Lutetiae Parisiorum, (1909) II, III. Hereafter cited as *De Religiosis.*

[9] Const. *"Cum ad regularem,"* 19 mart. 1603, § 20—*Fontes,* n. 189.

[10] Const. *"Cum ad regularem,"* 19 mart. 1603, § 20: ". . . ibique permaneant [novitii professi] quousque ad aetatem Sacris Ordinibus suscipiendis sufficientem devenerint, vel saltem per triennium post professionem, quo etiam tempore poterunt, quinimmo, et debebunt literarum studiis operam navare, sub directione, ac regimine *Superioris,* qui eas qualitates habeat, quibus Novitiorum Magistrum praeditum esse oportere dictum est."—*Fontes,* N. 189. Italics inserted in the text by the writer.

separated from that part of the house in which the novices as well as the older professed religious resided. If this plan was not followed, so that the professed students were sent to a monastery which did not serve as a novitiate, they followed a community life somewhat stricter than the one observed by the older professed religious.[11]

The length of *time* the priest was to continue his training of the students was also determined by the Clementine constitution. The spiritual training of the young professed was ordered to be carried on up to the time that sacred orders were received, or at least for three years after profession. During this period the students were forbidden to exercise any office connected with the administration of the monastery or with the external works of the ministry.[12]

Article III. From the Constitution "Cum ad regularem" to the Code

The Sacred Congregation of the Council, receiving special faculties from Urban VIII (1623–1644), renewed all the general decrees of Clement VIII concerning the reformation of Regulars, and the reception, profession and training of the novices.[13] However, there remained a doubt whether the Constitution *Cum ad regularem* was included in the legislation of the Sacred Congregation of the Council.[14] From that time to the Code there was no general pronouncement of the Church in regard to the priest caring for the spiritual life of clerics in religious institutes.

At the end of the nineteenth century and at the beginning of the twentieth two distinct situations presented themselves in religious Orders, demanding that a priest be appointed to a position similar to the one constituted by Clement VIII. One involved those who temporarily left the monastery in order to pursue further studies; the other pertained to those who returned to the monastery after spending a period of time in military service.

---

[11] *Loc. cit.*

[12] *Loc. cit.*

[13] S.C.C., decr., 21 sept. 1624—*Fontes,* n. 2454.

[14] Wernz, *Ius Decretalium,* III, 376, n. (262); Vermeersch, *De Religiosis,* II, III.

Pope Leo XIII (1878–1903) in 1896 sent an instruction to the Bishops and Superiors of religious Orders in Italy encouraging higher studies among clerics, and presenting norms for the guidance of individuals engaged in study. The religious were required frequently to visit a religious Superior of a nearby house or some other person outstanding in virtue and knowledge. The one who thus assumed the care of a clerical student was required to give a report on the religious to his Superior.[15] Pope Pius X (1903–1914) extended this instruction to the whole world.[16]

In 1911 the Sacred Congregation of Religious issued a decree concerning those recently returned to the monastery after a period of time spent in military service. The clerical religious in an order of Regulars had to return directly and immediately to the religious house. After a retreat, he was to be placed among the junior clerics under the special direction and vigilance of a priest commendable for prudence and piety. The Superior of the house and the priest in charge of the clerical students were required to report to the major Superior on the religious life of such a cleric.[17]

---

[15] S. C. Ep. et Reg., instr., 21 iul. 1896—*Fontes*, n. 2031.

[16] Pius X, litt. encycl. "*Pascendi,*" 8 sept. 1907—*Fontes*, n. 680.

[17] S. C. de Religiosis, decr., 1 ian. 1911—*Fontes*, n. 4408.

PART II

CANONICAL COMMENTARY

THE TITLE "SPIRITUAL PREFECT"

The priest to whom the duties of canon 588, § 1, are entrusted does not always possess the same title in the various religious clerical institutes. In some communities he is called " The Prefect of Scholastics "[1] or the " Praefectus Studentium,"[2] while the titles " Magister studentium,"[3] " Master "[4] and " Spiritual Director "[5] have been bestowed upon him in other religious institutes. Canon 588, §§ 1, 2 uses " Praefectus seu Magister spiritus."

In choosing for this study a general title taken from canon 588, one should prefer that which follows more closely the terminology of the canon and at the same time conveys the idea of the office as expressed in the common law. Augustine[6] uses the term " Prefect," but this is not a happy choice to designate the religious to whom are assigned the duties of canon 588, § 1, for such a title emphasizes the external discipline and might easily convey the notion that external discipline exclusively pertained to the office.

---

[1] *Regulae et Constitutiones Congregationis Sancti Spiritus sub tutela Immaculati Cordis Beatissimae Virginis Mariae* (Norwalk, Conn., 1934), nn. 463–467.

[2] *Constitutiones Ordinis Fratrum Beatissimae Virginis Mariae de Monte Carmelo* (Typis Polyglottis Vaticanis, 1930), nn. 331–333.

[3] *Regula Primitiva et Constitutiones Fratrum Discalceatorum Ordinis Sanctissimae Trinitatis Redemptionis Captivorum* (Isola del Liri: Soc. Tip. A. Macioce & Pisani, 1933), nn. 337–343.

[4] *The Rules and General Constitutions of the Friars Minor* (Paterson, N. J.: St. Anthony Guild Press, 1936), nn. 99–101.

[5] *The Constitutions of the Oblates of Saint Francis De Sales* (Translation published by the American Province, 1929), n. 43.

[6] *A Commentary on the New Code of Canon Law* (8 vols., St. Louis: Herder, Vol. III, 1919), III, 293.

The chief duty of the official under consideration is the spiritual formation of the students. Therefore, it is fitting that the word " spiritual " be a part of the title, as it is in the Code. The title " Spiritual Master " or " Spiritual Prefect " emphasizes the fact that the all important office to the incumbent of which it is applied is the training of the souls of the students, but at the same time it is sufficiently extensive to be applicable to the office when the external government of the students is also entrusted to this official by particular law. For this reason " Spiritual Master " or " Spiritual Prefect " is a better choice than " Spiritual Director," inasmuch as the latter term would be an incongruous designation of the office in the case in which the external rule is also entrusted to the person who has the spiritual formation of the students as his principal charge. But the title " Spiritual Prefect " will be preferred to " Spiritual Master " in this work in order to avoid all confusion which could arise from the frequent references that must be made to the Master of novices.

CHAPTER IV

THE AUTHORITY OF THE SPIRITUAL PREFECT

Article I. Preliminary Notions

A. EXPLANATION OF TERMS

In the treatment of the Spiritual Prefect it is necessary to explain not only the notion of certain terms, but also the juridical constitution of religious houses of studies. First attention will be paid to the explanation of terms.

1. External and Internal Superiors of Religious. The Superiors to whom religious are subject are of two kinds, first, those who are primarily constituted to exercise jurisdiction over the faithful, be they clerics, religious or laymen, and secondly, those who are members of a religious institute and are formally constituted to rule the religious according to the prescriptions of the religious rule.[1] The former are called the external Superiors of the religious, although their power may extend even to the internal forum, as in the case of the power of a Bishop to hear the confessions of women religious. These Superiors are the Pope, the Sacred Congregation of Religious and the local Ordinary. They are not members of the community, yet they possess power over the external and internal forums. On the other hand, the religious, members of the community, who are formally constituted to rule the institute, are called the internal Superiors of the religious. They are concerned solely with matters of their community and possess authority according to the norms of their constitutions. They are the Major and Minor religious Superiors.[2]

2. External and Internal Forums. The forum is the sphere in

[1] Berutti, *Institutiones Iuris Canonici* (6 vols., Taurini-Romae: Marietti, Vol. III, 1936), III, n. 21. Hereafter cited as *Institutiones.*

[2] Berutti, *Institutiones,* III, n. 21.

which certain matters are considered so to exist that they fall under one or another authority. To the external forum pertain primarily and essentially matters of the public and common good, the social actions which the faithful perform under the eye of the Church's public authority, not necessarily public actions as such, but actions which by their nature have a consequence for the perfect society, the Church.[3] Examples of matters belonging to the external forum are legislative, judicial and coercive power, the granting of faculties, public impediments and irregularities. In this group are also placed actions connected with the external rule of a community, such as elections and appointments to offices. Since they pertain to the external forum, they may be regulated either by jurisdictional or by dominative power.

The internal forum includes primarily and essentially the private good as opposed to the common good, and has regard to actions which have a relation to God alone, in conscience rather than in the cognizance which the church's public authority accords.[4] To this forum belong those matters which, either because they are occult by nature or in fact, touch men as individuals.[5] Hence, some actions belong to the internal forum because by their very nature they are occult, such as internal actions, thoughts, emotions, desires, while others are occult and belong to the internal forum inasmuch as they are unattended with any consideration or circumstantial implications for the public interest, as for instance, occult impediments and irregularities.[6] The confession of sins and the manifestation of conscience are acts pertaining to the internal forum. They refer primarily and essentially to the spiritual welfare of the individual. They disclose the innermost thoughts of the subject and treat of external actions from the viewpoint simply of sin. Preaching also belongs to the internal forum since it is primarily concerned with the spiritual welfare of individuals. Nevertheless the concession of the necessary faculties for preaching is an act of the

---

[3] Maroto, *Institutiones,* I, n. 719; Vermeersch-Creusen, *Epitome,* I, n. 313.

[4] Vermeersch-Creusen, *Epitome,* I. n. 313.

[5] Maroto, *Institutiones,* I, n. 271.

[6] Voltas, "De aperienda, directionis causa, Superioribus conscientia"—*Commentarium pro Religiosis,* I (1920), 55. Hereafter cited as *CpR.*

external forum, since its regulation is a matter involving the social good of the Church.[7]

3. Discipline. The term "discipline" ocurs frequently in the present law, but not always is it used in the same invariable sense. In some instances it refers to all those matters which fall under the power of jurisdiction, for instance, under the jurisdiction of the Sacred Congregation of the Council,[8] or of the Bishop.[9] In other places it pertains especially to those affairs which come under the dominative power as exercised in religious institutes.[10] In still other places it pertains to the matters of the novitiate which are referred to the power possessed by the Master of novices, and not to that possessed by the Ecclesiastical and Religious Superiors with their jurisdiction and dominative power.[11] As a consequence the term "discipline" cannot be said to signify jurisdiction only. It is a general term which must be understood according to the nature of the matter under consideration.

4. Regimen. *Regimen,* too, is a general term. It is used sometimes to mean jurisdiction, that is, the ruling power of the Church;[12] sometimes to signify dominative power, that is, the ruling power in a religious institute;[13] and again to indicate the power of the Master in the novitiate.[14] Therefore, the term must be understood according to the context of the canon and the nature of the matter involved.

B. THE CONSTITUTION OF HOUSES OF STUDIES

At the completion of the year of novitiate the professed clerical students are assigned to a house of studies where the common life should flourish in the utmost perfection.[15] The monastery designated for the house of studies is ruled by a local Superior, who possesses only dominative power in non-exempt re-

---

[7] Maroto, *Institutiones,* I, n. 722; Ottaviani, *Institutiones,* I, n. 120.

[8] Canon 250, § 1.

[9] Canon 336, § 2.

[10] Canons 499, § 2; 561, § 1; 618, § 2, 2°.

[11] Canons 562; 565, § 1.

[12] Canons 196; 334, § 2.

[13] Canons 618, § 2, 2°.

[14] Canon 561, § 1.

[15] Canon 587, §§ 1, 2.

ligious institutes, and both jurisdiction and dominative power in exempt religious institutes.[16] The authority of the local Superior extends over all the religious, priests, lay brothers, clerics in their studies, according to the Constitutions.[17] The local Superior has charge of those matters which concern the administration and the government of the monastery, matters which are of importance in the fulfillment of the purpose of the religious society. Among the duties of the Superior is the obligation of vigilance over the religious in matters which are spiritual, like the annual retreat, the duties of piety commanded by the particular law.[18] In the house of studies the local Superior has the obligation to insure in a special manner that the obligations of canon 595 are carried out with the greatest perfection.[19]

Confessors are to be assigned to each religious house of clerics according to canon 518, § 1. The house of studies is included under this prescription. Further, to the house of studies the Superiors are to send those religious who are exemplary in their zeal for the observance of the community regulations.[20] And, finally, the students are entrusted to the special care of the Spiritual Prefect who continues the spiritual formation of their souls.[21]

According to the pre-Code law the students were entrusted to the Spiritual Prefect, who was simply called a Superior, and the latter acted like the Master of novices in promoting the spiritual formation of the students and exercising the rule of the house of studies. He was responsible both for the spiritual formation of the students, and for the rule in community matters of that part of the monastery in which the students resided, although both he and the students were subject to the local Superior of the monastery.[22]

Does this juridical status continue in the present law, as Lan-

[16] Canon 501, § 1.

[17] Canon 502.

[18] Canon 595, §§§ 1, 2, 3.

[19] Canon 588, § 3.

[20] Canon 554, § 3.

[21] Canon 588, §§ 1, 2.

[22] Clement VIII, const. "*Cum ad regularem,*" 19 mart. 1603 § 20—*Fontes*, n. 189.

gasco [23] contends; or has there been a change in the pre-Code law resulting in the division of the office into two distinct assignments, spiritual authority and a disciplinary authority, as is proposed by Canuto; [24] or does the present law emphasize only the spiritual formation of the students, allowing the particular law to designate the person who takes care of disciplinary matters? To decide this question it will be necessary first to examine canon 588, in order to discover what charge is given to the Spiritual Prefect, and after that to determine whether he possesses any jurisdictional or dominative power.

ARTICLE II. RESTRICTION TO THE INTERNAL FORUM BY THE CODE

> Canon 588, § 1.—*Toto studiorum curriculo religiosi committantur speciali curae Praefecti seu Magistri spiritus qui eorum animos ad vitam religiosam informet opportunis monitis, instructionibus atque exhortationibus.*

The opinion adopted by the writer is that the influence of the Spiritual Prefect by reason of the present common law is limited to the sphere of the internal forum.

Canon 588, § 1, calls the official under consideration "Praefectus seu Magister spiritus," not "Praefectus" alone nor "Magister" alone. This title is an indication that the influence of the Spiritual Prefect is chiefly, although not exclusively, directed to the internal forum. His duty is to form character in the *souls* of the young religious, to promote their advancement in the *religious life.* The emphasis is placed in the canon on the spiritual good of *individuals.* This work of spiritual formation is to be accompanied by admonitions, instructions and exhortations, not by precepts which require at least the possession of dominative power.[25]

---

[23] "De regimine domus studiorum in religione clericali"—*JP,* XVIII (1938), 118–131; XIX (1939), 55–69, 191–201.

[24] "De regimine domus studiorum in religione clericali exempta ad normam can. 588"—*Apollinaris,* IX (1936), 19–39.

[25] Coronata, *Institutiones Iuris Canonici ad Usum Utriusque Cleri et Scholarum* (5 vols., Taurini [Italia]: Marietti, 1928–1936), I, n. 597. Hereafter cited as *Institutiones,*

Admonitions, instructions and exhortations are acts which are restricted by the canon to the internal forum inasmuch as it emphasizes the spiritual advancement of the students. To use these means to form the character of the students is to act in the same manner as the pastor who delivers a sermon to the people for their instruction and improvement The action of the latter is one which pertains to the internal forum.[26] Furthermore, the discipline and government of the house of studies are not mentioned as entrusted to the Spiritual Prefect in the way in which the government of the novitiate, and not merely the spiritual training of the novices, is committed to the care of the Master of novices.[27]

The students are entrusted to the " special care " of the Spiritual Prefect. In itself " special care " does not postulate either the external forum or the internal forum, but must be understood from the context of the canon, as is the case with words like " regimen " and " discipline," which do not always have the same meaning. The " special care " must be understood along with the other words of the canon. And since it is the spiritual formation of the students that is emphasized in the remaining part of the canon, it must be to that that the " special care " refers.

From the foregoing considerations it seems that the role assigned to the Spiritual Prefect by reason of the common law is only the spiritual training of the students. The title "*Praefectus seu Magister spiritus*" indicates that his chief work is a spiritual one. The duties assigned him by the canon require only that through him souls be formed in the religious life. The religious perfection of the individual, not the government and discipline of the house of studies, constitutes the charge entrusted to him.

The authors treat the problem of the Spiritual Prefect's authority with the utmost caution. Only Wernz (1842–1914)—Vidal (1867–1938),[28] Canuto,[29] Berutti,[30] and Larraona [31] speak

---

[26] Maroto, *Institutiones*, I, n. 721.

[27] Canon 561, § 1: ". . . ad ipsumque unum novitiatus regimen spectat."

[28] *Ius Canonicum ad Codicis Normam exactum* (7 vols., in 8, Romae: apud Aedes Universitatis Gregorianae, 1923–1938, Vol. III, 1933), III, n. 332. Hereafter cited as *Ius Canonicum*.

openly *in favor of* the opinion which limits the Spiritual Prefect's influence to the internal forum. On the other hand, only Goyeneche,[32] Schaefer [33] and Langasco [34] make any open declaration against it.

Chelodi (1880–1922),[35] Cappello [36] and Ferreres (1861–1936) [37] simply quote the canon, or express the idea of the canon in similar words. Raus,[38] Cocchi [39] and Prummer (1866–1931) [40] emphasize that the duty of the Spiritual Prefect is the spiritual formation of the students. None of these authors advances the opinion that any authority in the external forum is entrusted to the Spiritual Prefect by reason of the common law. But likewise they do not deny the fact. Consequently one can conclude from their writings that the spiritual training is entrusted to the Spiritual Prefect, but no conclusion can be reached as regards his power in the external forum.

Pejška [41] says that the authority of the Spiritual Prefect is

---

[29] "De regimine domus studiorum in religione clericali exempta ad normam can. 588"—*Apollinaris,* IX (1936), 19–39.

[30] *Institutiones,* III, n. 100.

[31] "*Consultationes*"—*CpR,* I (1920), 53 (6).

[32] "*Consultationes*"—*CpR,* VII (1926), 183.

[33] *De Religiosis ad Normam Codicis Iuris Canonici* (3 ed., Romae: S.A.L.E.R., 1940), p. 635. Hereafter cited as *De Religiosis.*

[34] "De regimine domus studiorum in religione clericali"—*JP,* XIX (1939), 55–69, 191–201.

[35] *Ius de Personis,* n. 275.

[36] *Summa Iuris Canonici in Usum Scholarum Concinnata* (3 vols., Romae: apud Aedes Universitatis Gregorianae, vol. II, 3. ed., 1939), II, n. 619. Hereafter cited as *Summa Iuris Canonici.*

[37] *Institutiones Canonicae* (2. ed., 2 vols., Barcinonae, 1920), I, n. 883. Hereafter cited as *Institutiones.*

[38] *Institutiones Canonicae iuxta Novum Codicem Iuris pro scholis* vel ad usum privatum syntheticae redactae (2. ed., Lugduni: Vitte, 1931), p. 313. Hereafter cited as *Institutiones.*

[39] *Commentarium in Codicem Iuris Canonici"* (8 vols., Taurinorum Augustae Marietti, vol., IV, 3. ed., 1932), IV, n. 87. Hereafter cited as *Commentarium.*

[40] *Manuale Iuris Ecclesiasticae* (3 ed., Friburgi Brisgoviae: Herder, 1922), p. 288. Hereafter cited as *Manuale.*

[41] *Ius Canonicum Religiosorum* (3. ed., Friburgi Brisgoviae: Herder, (1927), p. 163. Hereafter cited as *Ius Canonicum.*

more limited than that of the Master of novices. This statement can be interpreted to mean that the Spiritual Prefect has no authority in the external forum, or that he has some but not as much as is possessed by the Master of novices. Vermeersch (1858–1936)-Creusen[42] remark that if the exterior discipline is committed to the Spiritual Prefect, it is contrary to the mind of the Code for him to hear the confessions of the students. But one may ask from what source would such external authority arise? If from the particular law or from a delegation by the Superior, then it is clear that the opinion of Vermeersch-Creusen would be in favor of the non-possession of authority in the external forum by reason of the common law. Such seems to be the opinion for they say that there is no prohibition against the Spiritual Prefect acting as ordinary confessor to the students.

Wernz-Vidal[43] are unmistakably clear in their statement on the question of the authority of the Spiritual Prefect. They say that the commission of this office is confined to the internal spiritual care of souls, and that in this formation the Spiritual Prefect can be aided by spiritual exercises of piety, even external exercises by which the internal spirit is nourished. According to them canon 588, § 1, does not treat of the external government. That, they say, pertains to the Superior of the monastery, and not to the Spiritual Prefect.

Berutti follows the same opinion. He cites the Clementine Constitution *Cum ad regularem,* and then states that its prescription flourishes today in some religious institutes by reason of their Constitutions. But the only requirement of the common law he holds to be canon 588, § 1, which he then proceeds to quote. Thus he clearly states that there is a change in the present law from that of Clement VIII. He concludes by saying that the Spiritual Prefect must receive his power from some other source than the common law if he is to rule the students in the same manner that the Master of novices rules the novices.[44] This same idea is consistently followed in his treatment of the manifestation of conscience to which canon 530 adverts, namely, that only from

[42] *Epitome,* I, n. 741.

[43] *Ius Canonicum,* III, n. 332.

[44] *Institutiones,* III, n. 100.

particular law does the Spiritual Prefect have the external government of the students.[45]

Canuto, too, maintains that the Spiritual Prefect has charge only of the spiritual formation of the students. His arguments are drawn from the words of canon 588, and from the present practice of the Church which favors a separation of the forums.[46] It is his first argument that has the greater weight, for he seems to overstress the second argument, forgetting that the practice of the Church in regard to the separation of the forum is not so absolute as never to allow any intermingling of the forums.[47]

Finally, Larraona, in treating of the question of the Master hearing the confessions of the novices, says that the Spiritual Prefect is not embraced by the prescriptions of canon 891, neither is the Master himself included under the scope of the canon if he exercises the office of Spiritual Prefect and hears the confessions of the professed, as is done in some institutes. The reason he gives is that the external discipline is not necessarily entrusted to the Spiritual Prefect by common law as it is in the case of the Master of novices. Nevertheless, he admits that sometimes from particular law the external discipline is included in the charge of the Spiritual Prefect. In such an instance the Spiritual Prefect is more like a Superior than a Master of novices. Although Larraona is expressly treating the question of confession of the novices, yet in his discussion he touches on the point of the Spiritual Prefect's authority.[48]

In summarizing the views of the authors, one makes the following observations. Concerning the limits of the authority of the Spiritual Prefect authors proceed with the utmost caution.

---

[45] *Institutiones,* III, n. 55.

[46] "De regimine domus studiorum in religione clericali exempta ad normam can. 588"—*Apollinaris,* IX (1936), 19–22.

[47] Cf. *infra,* pp. 92–94; also canons 518, § 2, 530, § 2.

[48] "Consultationes"—*CpR,* I (1920), 53, (6): "Ita ex littera legis patet, sed et ratio favet cum ex iure generali in Praefecto spiritus necessario non adsit, ut in Magistro, potestas illa disciplinaris quae ad externum regimen novitiatus necessaria est (c. 561): quando vero ex iure particulari, Praefectus spiritus insimul curat de regimine externo, potius Superiori religioso aequiparandus videretur, etsi. . . ."

Some quote canon 588, § 1, verbatim, or use similar words.[49] Others emphasize the spiritual formation of the students,[50] while Pejška speaks of the Spiritual Prefect as having a power more limited than that of the Master of novices.[51] Coronata [52] forbids the Spiritual Prefect to hear the confessions of the students if the exterior discipline is granted to him. He uses the word "*augeatur*" to describe the situation when the Spiritual Prefect is entrusted with authority in the external forum. This word implies that the concession of external authority comes from particular law or from delegation, and hence that the Spiritual Prefect lacks such power according to the prescriptions of the common law. Berutti,[53] Canuto,[54] Wernz-Vidal,[55] Larraona [56] and Vermeersch-Creusen [57] assert that the Spiritual Prefect has no authority in the external forum. Coronata clearly implies that he maintains the same opinion.

On the opposite side are Langasco,[58] Goyeneche [59] and Schaefer.[60] Goyeneche considers the present law to be a continuation of the law of Clement VIII.[61] According to this Constitution a priest with the title of Superior had entrusted to him both the spiritual formation of the students and the government of the house of studies. He acted as instructor and disciplinarian. In opposition to the view just stated, however, one observes that while the present law clearly places the students under the care

---

[49] Chelodi, *Ius de Personis*, n. 275; Cappello, *Summa Iuris Canonici*, II, n. 619; Ferreres, *Institutiones*, I, n. 883.

[50] Cocchi, *Commentarium*, IV, n. 87; Raus, *Institutiones*, p. 313; Prummer, *Manuale*, p. 288.

[51] *Ius Canonicum*, p. 163.

[52] *Institutiones*, I, n. 597.

[53] *Institutiones*, III, n. 100.

[54] " De regimine domus studiorum in religione clericali exempta ad normam can. 588 "—*Apollinaris*, IX (1936), 19-39.

[55] *Ius Canonicum*, III, n. 332.

[56] " Consultationes "—*CpR*, I (1920), 63 (6).

[57] *Epitome*, I, n. 741.

[58] " De regimine domus studiorum in religione clericali "—*JP*, XIX (1939), 55-69, 191-201.

[59] " Consultationes "—*CpR*, VII (1926), 183.

[60] *De Religiosis*, p. 635.

[61] Const., "*Cum ad regularem*," 19 mart. 1603, § 20—*Fontes*, n. 189.

of the Spiritual Prefect for spiritual training, it is very difficult to prove from the canon that the external rule of the house of studies has also been put in his charge.

Langasco says that the house of studies has always been considered somewhat like a novitiate, and has had a priest to form the spiritual life of the students and to take charge of the discipline of the house of studies.[62] To this objection it may be answered that the same condition may continue today if the Spiritual Prefect is given the necessary concession of authority by delegation or particular law. But it still is to be proved that such a concession is contained in canon 588, § 1.

Again, Langasco states that if the Spiritual Prefect is to train the students spiritually with profit, he needs some disciplinary power over them, and that in fact such is implied in the terms of canon 588, § 1, namely, in the phrases "*speciali curae*" and "*monitis, instructionibus atque exhortationibus.*"[63] In reply to this objection it may be stated that whatever is implied in the phrases "*speciali curae*" and "*monitis, instructionibus atque exhortationibus*" is directed toward the principal work of the Spiritual Prefect—the individual's spiritual life. Furthermore, the Spiritual Director in the diocesan seminary has a similar task of forming the souls of the clerics, and his task is limited to the internal forum.[64]

Concerning the house of studies with its strict observance of the common life, its separation from the part of the monastery in which the priests reside, its emphasis on the training of the students, one notes a similarity between it and the novitiate. Furthermore, the spiritual training of the students in many cases can be accomplished with greater profit if at the same time the external discipline is entrusted to the Spiritual Prefect. From a consideration of the authors, the nature of the constitution of a religious house of study, and of the wording of canon 588, the following is the conclusion of the writer. Canon 588, § 1, has

[62] "De regimine domus studiorum in religione clericali"—*JP*, XVIII (1938), 125.

[63] Langasco, "De regimine domus studiorum in religione clericali"—*JP*, XIX (1939), 57.

[64] Canon 1358.

entrusted one duty to the Spiritual Prefect—the spiritual formation of the students. At the same time the canon has left to each institute the matter of deciding to whom the external government of the students will be entrusted, whether to the Superior of the house, his Assistant, the Master of novices, the Prefect of Studies, the lectors or the Spiritual Prefect. Thus the long standing customs and regulations of each institute are preserved, the canon under consideration is observed, and the spiritual training of the students is assured.

Article III. Lack of Jurisdiction and Dominative Power

A. Jurisdiction

1. *External Forum*

Jurisdiction in the external forum is exercised primarily and directly for the social good of the Church, and only secondarily and indirectly for the good of the individual.[65] But since the authority of the Spiritual Prefect is primarily and directly ordained for the good of the individual as shown in the preceding Article, he has no power in the external forum and possesses no jurisdiction in the external forum.

2. *Internal Extra-sacramental Forum*

Canon 1328 states that no one shall exercise the ministry of preaching unless he receives a canonical mission from a legitimate Superior, or has an office in which the duty of preaching inheres. The discharge of the office of preaching to the faithful is sometimes reduced to an exercise of jurisdiction in the internal non-sacramental forum.[66] Now, Canon 588, § 1, states that the Spiritual Prefect of the students shall train the clerical students in the religious life, and this duty is to be accomplished by counsels, exhortations and instructions. Must we conclude, then, that just as the cleric who exercises the office of preaching to the faithful needs jurisdiction in the internal non-sacramental forum, so too the Spiritual Prefect must have the same jurisdiction to impart the proper instructions to the students?

[65] Ottaviani, *Institutiones,* I, n. 120.

[66] Maroto, *Institutiones,* n. 721. Ottaviani, *Institutiones,* I, n. 120.

It is not required that the Spiritual Prefect possess jurisdiction in the internal non-sacramental forum, for his duty is attached to a private position in an imperfect society. He does not act as an officially appointed minister of the Church, but as an official representative of an imperfect society. He is sent to a religious institute and acts as a member of that institute. His work is accomplished in a manner similar to that of the Master of novices. The latter instructs and prepares the novices for religious profession by means of his exhortations and instructions on the religious life and the Rule of the community. This duty is also performed in communities of women religious by the Mistress of novices. Since this work can be done by women as well as by men lay religious, who certainly possess no jurisdiction in any forum, so too the instructions in clerical institutes can be given by the Spiritual Prefect without any jurisdiction from the proper Ordinary. His assignment is not unlike that of lay persons who assist the pastor, under certain conditions, in the catechetical instruction of the children.[67] Those giving instructions in the latter case do not require jurisdiction, for they do not act in an official capacity, that is, as a public minister of the Church. Likewise the office of Spiritual Prefect, although sanctioned and approved by the Church, is one that exists in an imperfect society, and the incumbent is not commissioned as a public minister in the name of the Church, but as an official instructor of the religious society. It is, therefore, safe to conclude that the priest filling the capacity of Spiritual Prefect does not have jurisdiction in the internal non-sacramental forum by reason of the common law.

3. *Internal Sacramental Forum*

The Spiritual Prefect is not the ordinary confessor of the students by reason of the common law. Consequently, he does not possess jurisdiction in the internal sacramental forum by reason of his office. The treatment of the question of confession as it concerns the Spiritual Prefect will be deferred until a later chapter. If the Spiritual Prefect is appointed confessor to the students, his jurisdiction in the internal sacramental forum proceeds not from his office, but from delegation.

[67] Canon 1333, § 1.

B. DOMINATIVE POWER

It has been maintained in the foregoing that the Spiritual Prefect has no jurisdiction in the external and internal forum by reason of his office. Does he exercise any dominative power over the students?

The answer must likewise be that the Spiritual Prefect by reason of his office has no dominative power over the clerical students. His work is restricted to directing and nurturing the internal life of the souls of the religious. He does not have any disciplinary power, and the government of the students is not entrusted to him. In no place in the Code is he called a Superior, and authors refrain from applying that title to him. Furthermore, Canon 501, § 1, states that Superiors and Chapters, according to the Constitutions and the common law, have dominative power over their subjects. Unless the Constitutions expressly give this power to the Spiritual Prefect, he does not possess it, since the common law does not grant it.

Since the Spiritual Prefect does not possess any dominative power, he is not able to nullify the private vows of the religious in clerical institutes.[68]

---

[68] Canon 1312, § 1.

CHAPTER V

THE OFFICE OF THE SPIRITUAL PREFECT

Article I. Nature of the Office

The Spiritual Prefect exercises an office, but an office in the wide sense of the term. Canon 145, § 1, states that an ecclesiastical office in the wide sense is any position, any employment legitimately exercised for a spiritual purpose. An ecclesiastical office in the strict sense is any stable and fixed position, created either by divine or ecclesiastical law, conferred according to the norms of canon law, and carrying with it some participation of power, whether of orders or of jurisdiction. Canon 145, § 2, prevents difficulties from arising in regard to the interpretation of the word *office* in any particular canon of the Code by stating that this term must be taken in the strict sense unless the context demands that it be taken in a wide sense.

The position of the Spiritual Prefect is a stable and fixed one, created by ecclesiastical authority and sanctioned by the law of canon 588, §§ 1, 2. But it does not promote the incumbent to higher orders, nor does it give him the right to exercise any latent powers of sacred orders, as occurs when an ordained cleric in priestly orders is made a pastor. Likewise by the common law the Spiritual Prefect does not possess jurisdiction, either in the external forum [1] or, as it seems, in the internal extra-sacramental forum. As to the latter, it has been shown that a Mistress of novices in institutes of women religious enjoys the analogous power of instructing her charges without possessing any jurisdiction over them. Furthermore, the Spiritual Prefect exercises his office not as a public minister, but as a member and representative of an imperfect society, although his office is sanctioned and approved by the perfect society, the Church.[2] The office of the Spiritual Prefect does not carry with it jurisdiction even

[1] Cf. supra, p. 40.

[2] Cf. supra, pp. 40, 41.

in the internal sacramental forum, inasmuch as its incumbent is not the official confessor for the religious students. The Spiritual Prefect becomes their confessor only when he receives an appointment by the proper authority and with it, the requisite jurisdiction.

Hence, though the Spiritual Prefect has an office, it is an office in the wide sense of the term. His duty or employment requires that he form the souls of the clerical students and direct them toward a spiritual end—their own religious perfection. Thus it is that his commission fulfills the conditions postulated for an office in the wide sense of the term, namely, the exercise of an employment for a spiritual purpose.[3] It is not necessary that the Code explicitly call a certain position an office in order that it be juridically recognized as evincing those essential traits and factors which constitute it as an office in either the strict or wide sense of the word. It is sufficient that factually the position does evince whatever is postulated as essential for an office. Thus the position of sacristan, while it is not mentioned in the Code, is obviously an office in the wide sense.[4]

Article II. Incompatible Offices and Duties

A. Incompatible Offices

The position assigned to the Spiritual Prefect is considered an office in the wide sense of the term, since it is exercised for a spiritual end, namely, the formation of the souls of the students. It is forbidden to give to the Spiritual Prefect any other office besides this office of the spiritual direction of the junior religious if the secondary assignment interferes with his principal assignment. Canon 559, § 3, states that the Master of novices is prohibited from assuming any offices and duties which are incompatible with the care and the rule of the novices. Canon 588, § 2, refers to canon 559, § 3, and makes the latter canon applicable to the Spiritual Prefect, due allowance being made for any difference in their offices, in their subjects and in their duties. To determine in the concrete which particular offices cannot with legal compati-

[3] Canon 145, § 1.

[4] Vermeersch-Creusen, *Epitome*, I, n. 227.

bility be exercised simultaneously, it is necessary to consider the nature of the offices, the prescriptions of general and particular law, and finally, the juridical directives inherent in laudably received customs.[5]

In some religious institutes the Constitutions indicate the offices which may not be simultaneously conferred on the same religious. In some instances the established customs of the religious community serve as a guide for those who are entrusted with the duty of making the appointments. Generally, the office of *major Superior* is incompatible with that of the Spiritual Prefect on account of the numerous duties inherent in the former office, the difference of residence normally connected with the incumbencies in these two offices. By common law the *local Superior* is not forbidden to act also as the Spiritual Prefect, if the office of the latter is considered as it exists according to the common law. The Spiritual Prefect has entrusted to him by common law the spiritual formation of the students. Yet he is not necessarily a confessor for them. For that status he needs a special appointment from the proper Superior. Likewise the students are not under any obligation to make a manifestation of conscience to the Spiritual Prefect. Thus in a small community the same religious could quite conceivably fulfill at the same time the roles of local Superior and Spiritual Prefect. But if he does assume both offices, namely, to promote the spiritual formation of the students by instructions, exhortations and admonitions, and to accomplish also the duties joined to the external government of the community, he is strictly bound by the laws enacted in canons 518 and 530. For though he is the Spiritual Prefect, he is also the Superior, and for this specific reason must proceed according to the prescripts of the canons dealing with the question of the confession of sins and of the manifestation of conscience. If the duties of the government of the monastery are so weighty that the local Superior is occupied constantly in the faithful discharge of them, then from the very lack of time and opportunity for assuming the execution of additional duties he is excluded from simultaneously exercising the second office, namely, the office of

[5] Wernz-Vidal, *Ius Canonicum,* II, n. 214.

Spiritual Prefect. The size of the monastery, the number of religious, the quantity and frequency of the appointments and assignments, are factors which one must consider in judging of the incompatibility of the offices of the local Superior and Spiritual Prefect as determined by the common law.

If the Spiritual Prefect has the external government of the students entrusted to him, he exercises a charge similar to that of the Master of novices, and consequently is bound in the same manner by the law of canon 559, § 3, as the Master of novices. Larraona[6] states that canon 559, § 3, is derived from the pre-Code law, has its authority from that source, and hence must be considered according to the received interpretations of the approved authors. He asserts that neither the authors nor the Constitutions of religious institutes in general acknowledged the existence of an absolute incompatibility between the offices of the Master of novices and the local Superior, although he admits that the Constitutions of religious communities usually did presuppose the separation of the offices, and readily grants that factually the joining of the offices in one and the same person occurred only infrequently. When the simultaneous exercise of both offices by the same religious does occur, then, so he states, the case is one in which the monastery serves simply for a novitiate with its members.

If the Spiritual Prefect has authority in the external forum so that he exercises his office in the same manner as the Master of novices, the same rules prevail. There is no absolute incompatibility between his office and that of the local Superior, and therefore, in a house of studies which has no members except the students, the local Superior could also be appointed as Spiritual Prefect.

It is not forbidden to the Spiritual Prefect, though he is entrusted with the spiritual formation of the students by common law, to receive a share in the external government of the students in the house of studies. This is both the theory and practice in some religious institutes which have received full pontifical approbation for their Constitutions since the promulgation of the

---

[6] " Consultationes "—*CpR,* II (1921), 291, 292.

Code.[7] Those who act as lectors for the students are not forbidden by the common law to assume the office of Spiritual Prefect. The number of clerics in the monastery together with the frequency of the classes must be taken into account by the Superior when he considers entrusting the students to the spiritual care of the lector.

B. INCOMPATIBLE DUTIES

Particular law of the institute and custom will determine in specific instances the assignments that may not be given to the Spiritual Prefect. Larraona,[8] in treating of duties which are incompatible with the official duties of the Master of novices, states that duties which call the Master away from the monastery are prohibited. Likewise, those occupations are forbidden to the Master, he says, which not only occupy the time that should be bestowed on the novices, but also are a source of distraction from his principal work in that they dissipate the physical energies of body and soul. In like manner it may be said that any employments which directly or indirectly interfere with the proper exercise of the office of the Spiritual Prefect are forbidden. Such employments are forbidden with greater or lesser strictness according as they interfere in greater or lesser measure with the attainment of his principal duty.

Occasional and brief absences from the monastery in the discharge of the works of the institute will not necessarily interfere with the training of the students, but can rather serve to increase the fruitfulness of the Spiritual Prefect's work, for the experience gathered can aid him in the direction of the students and provide him with concrete proof of the dangers that may arise on the occasion of the performance of the work of the religious society. It must be emphasized, however, that the absences, if justified in an exceptional case, must be brief and infrequent.

Preaching assignments and confessional appointments fulfilled

---

[7] *Regula Primitiva et Constitutiones Fratrum Discalceatorum Ordinis Sanctissimae Trinitatis Redemptionis Captivorum,* nn. 337–343; *Constitutiones Ordinis Fratrum Minorum Sancti Patris Francisci Conventualium* (Romae: Ad SS. XII Apostolos, 1932), n. 161.

[8] "Consultationes"—*CpR,* II (1921), 294.

in the hours during which the students are engaged in study are not incompatible with the duties of the Spiritual Prefect, provided that the preparation for preaching and confession does not occupy such long hours as to interfere with the principal work of training the students spiritually. If an assignment required several days of preparation during the hours which should be given to the care of the students, it would be a duty incompatible with that of the Spiritual Prefect's office, even though the ultimate execution of the assignment required only a few hours' absence from the monastery. The Spiritual Prefect should be present in the monastery on days when the students are free from classes, for instance, on Sundays and feast days, so that he will be accessible to those who are entrusted to his care.

The local Superior is entrusted with the rule of the monastery, and accordingly assigns the duties to the religious, including the Spiritual Prefect. He is the ordinary judge of the incompatible duties, being guided by the prescriptions of common and particular law. To ensure a correct judgment regarding the compatibility of the duties which he assigns to the Spiritual Prefect, the local Superior should have a thorough understanding of the principal duties of the Spiritual Prefect, so that other assignments given to the Spiritual Prefect by the Superior will not interfere with the duties attached to the office by the common or particular law. The Spiritual Prefect must abide by the judgment of the local Superior, but he still is free to interpose a recourse to the major Superiors when the extraneous duties assigned to him by the local Superior seem to impede the exercise of the duties committed to him by the common law of the Code or the particular law of the institute.

Article III. The Appointment of the Spiritual Prefect

The Code does not specify the Superior who is to appoint the Spiritual Prefect. In the absence of such legislation, it is necessary to have recourse to particular law, that is, to the Constitutions and customs of the religious institute. When the particular law designates the Superior who is to make the appointment, the prescription is to be followed. If the Constitutions and customs of a religious institute do not provide for the appointment of the

Spiritual Prefect, then it will be necessary to search for a general principle in the particular law, namely, to discover if the appointments to all or to certain types of offices in the community are left to the General Superior or to the Provincial Superior. If the Constitutions are entirely silent in the matter of such appointments, then it seems that the appointment is to be made by the General Superior if the Spiritual Prefect exercises his office in a house of studies which admits students of the entire religious institute, and by the Provincial Superior when the house of studies is open only to the students of the province.

This last statement is justified by the following reasons. Canon 587, § 3, states that, if a religious institute, or province within the institute, is not able to have a house of studies, certain alternatives are allowed the Superior. From the use of the words "*religio vel provincia*" by the legislator, it seems that the house of studies is considered as a matter which primarily concerns the province, or also the institute if there is a general house of studies. Consequently, it is the Superior with authority over the institute or province who is competent in the matter of supervising the house of studies and of providing for the appointment of its officials. Again, the office of the Spiritual Prefect is such by nature as to have effects not only for the monastery in which the incumbent resides, but also for the entire province for which he trains the students. These reasons, then, seem adequate warrant for the conclusion that, when the Constitutions are silent in this matter, the Provincial Superior is authorized to appoint the Spiritual Prefect for the house of studies which serves only the province, and the General Superior for the house of studies designated for the entire institute.

Furthermore, if the Constitutions are silent, the General or Provincial Superiors respectively do not need the consent or advice of the Council or Chapter in making the appointment. If the consent of others is required, this requirement must be followed for the validity of the appointment. If it is necessary only that their advice be obtained, then that advice must be sought for the validity of the appointment, though it need not be followed.

There are, however, some auhors[9] who consider the Superior's act of appointment to be valid, though of course they condemn it as illicit, when even the required seeking of the advice has not been accomplished.

Article IV. Duration of the Office

There is no law in the Code to determine the duration of the office of the Spiritual Prefect. Hence the norms are to be sought in the Constitutions and established customs of the respective religious institutes. There is no prohibition arising from the common law—even if the Spiritual Prefect possesses authority over the students in the external forum—which forbids tenure of the office for a long period of time. Since the work of the Spiritual Prefect is analogous to that of the Master of novices rather than to that of the local Superior, the Superiors seem to be acting in fundamental harmony with the spirit of the law when they keep a competent man in office for a long period of time.[10]

Article V. Power of Dispensing

A. From the Common Law of the Church

Since the Spiritual Prefect has no jurisdiction by reason of his office, he is not able to grant a dispensation except in those cases for which he receives express delegation from the proper ecclesiastical authority.[11] He cannot dispense the students in religious institutes from the general laws of the Church, not even from the laws in regard to fast and abstinence. In clerical exempt institutes the power to dispense from the law of fast and abstinence is granted to the major and minor Superiors. It is exercised by them over their subjects in the same manner it is exercised by the pastor within the confines of his authority.[12] This power as enjoyed by the Superiors in clerical exempt religious communities

---

[9] Vermeersch-Creusen, *Epitome,* I, n. 197; Wernz-Vidal, *Ius Canonicum* (Vol. II [De Personis] 2. ed., 1928), II, n. 33, (3); Boudinhon, "An nullus semper sit actus Superioris non petito consilio?"—*JP,* VIII (1928), 29-35.

[10] Canon 560.

[11] Canon 80.

[12] Canon 1245, § 3.

is an ordinary power, for it is possessed by them through the office to which the common law has attached this power.[13]

Canon 199, § 1, states that ordinary power may be delegated totally or partially unless the law expressly makes a provision to the contrary. Since in the law there is not any prohibition against a superior's act of delegating to others his own power to dispense his subjects from the law of fast and abstinence, he may delegate this power to the Spiritual Prefect. The latter, if he receives the power of dispensing in the same fulness in which it is enjoyed by the Superior, may dispense not only individual students for a just cause according to the rule of canon 1245, §§ 1, 3, but also the students as a group, if in the same community a sufficient number of novices or priests reside to constitute a distinct group from the students, for in this case the students do not constitute the entire community in the monastery, but only a part of the community, and thus they may be likened to a family in a parish.[14]

Religious Superiors in non-exempt religious communities have no power under the common law to dispense from the ecclesiastical law of fast and abstinence. If the Spiritual Prefect in such communities is to enjoy this power, it is necessary for him to obtain it from the Ordinary of the place. If the faculties of the diocese in which the religious house is located grant this power to all the priests, then the Spiritual Prefect with diocesan faculties is able to dispense from the law of fast and abstinence.

B. FROM THE CONSTITUTIONS

Sometimes in exempt and non-exempt religious communities there is a fast or an abstinence which is observed by reason of the Constitutions. The day of its observance may coincide with that of an ecclesiastical precept of fast or abstinence, or it may fall outside of any day on which the ecclesiastical precept binds in the same matter. On days when both the Constitutions and the

---

13 Canons 1245, § 3; 197, § 1.

14 Berutti, *Institutiones* (Vol. IV, De Rebus, Taurini-Romae: Marietti, 1940), IV, n. 60; Vermeersch-Creusen, *Epitome* (Vol. II, Mechliniae-Romae: Dessain, 1940), n. 556; Fanfani, *De Iure Religiosorum ad Normam Codicis Iuris Canonici* (2. ed., Taurini-Romae: Marietti, 1925), n. 53. Hereafter cited as *De Iure Religiosorum*.

ecclesiastical precept make fasting or abstinence obligatory, the Spiritual Prefect cannot dispense the students unless he has both the necessary delegation to dispense from the ecclesiastical precept and the authority to dispense from the obligation imposed by the rule of the institute. Thus it may happen that during Lent the religious are bound to observe a daily fast by reason of both the general law of the Church and the particular law of the religious community. If the Spiritual Prefect possessed the necessary power to dispense from the ecclesiastical precept, but not from the law of the institute, then the student religious could be dispensed from the latter obligation only by one who has the necessary authority from the Constitutions, or a proper delegation from the competent religious Superior. The Superior can therefore still insist on the observance of the law of the institute by such religious who have obtained a dispensation simply from the common law of the Church. However, the proper Superior will have no difficulty in finding sufficient cause to dispense from the rule. The fact that a just cause was present to dispense from the grave ecclesiastical precept indicates that a just cause is also present to dispense from the rule which ordinarily does not impose a serious obligation in this matter.

CHAPTER VI

THE QUALITIES OF THE SPIRITUAL PREFECT

Article I. The Qualities of the Superior of the Students in the Clementine Law

Clement VIII in his Constitution *Cum ad regularem* [1] ordered that a priest be appointed in institutes of Regulars to supervise the training of the clerical students. This priest was given the title of Superior. The qualities demanded of him coincided with the qualities required in the Master of novices. The Constitution did not specifically enumerate the qualities of the Superior of the students under the paragraph dealing with this official. It simply stated that the qualities required in the Master of novices were likewise required in the Superior of the students.[2] Consequently, under the law of Clement VIII the qualities required in the incumbents of both these offices were the same.

The first necessary quality was the Sacrament of Orders. The man chosen to be Superior of the students had to be a validly ordained priest. In the second place the priest appointed to the office was required to be " quinto saltem supra trigesimum aetatis suae anno constitutus." [3] What was the exact meaning of this phrase in the pre-Code law? Did this phrase point to the beginning of the thirty-fifth year or the completion of it?

Dubé, after studying the earlier law in its passages which mention the last year in any given series of years, concludes that the text of the law and not the nature of the office was accepted as the primary norm for determining whether the beginning or the completion of the last year was thus indicated as a requirement. He admits that an exception to this rule was applicable in the legal texts which dealt with appointment to benefices. In such

[1] 19 mart. 1603,—*Fontes,* n. 189.

[2] §§ 9, 20,—*Fontes,* n. 189.

[3] Const., "*Cum ad regularem,*" § 9,—*Fontes,* n. 189,

instances only the beginning of the last year of the series had to be reached. In other cases, if there was present in the text the ablative case or the prepositions "*iuxta*," "*in*," "*ad*," "*intra*," "*ante*," the beginning of the last year in a series of years was sufficient to constitute the requisite age. If, on the other hand, the genitive case, or the accusative case as governed by the prepositions "*per*" or "*post*," was written in the text, then the law postulated the lapse of the full duration of the year there indicated.[4]

In the text of the Constitution *Cum ad regularem* the word "*quinto*" stands without any preposition, and in the ablative case. There is no reason for departing from the ordinary manner of interpretation in this instance. Consequently the conclusion is that the beginning and not the completion of the thirty-fifth year was the age requirement for the position both of the Master of novices and of the Superior of the students.

Not many commentators discussed this point in any appreciable detail. Some, when they wrote on the Master of novices, were satisfied simply with quoting the text of the Constitution *Cum ad regularem*.[5] Bastien (1866–1940) expressly required the completion of the thirty-fifth year before the religious was eligible for the office of Master of novices.[6] Vermeersch, in his pre-Code writings, was more lenient than Bastien, and demanded only the beginning of the thirty-fifth year, not its completion.[7]

Another quality specified in the Constitution *Cum ad regularem* for the Superior of the students was his status of ten years' profession. The text contained the preposition "per."[8] According to the general principles for the computation of time in the pre-

---

[4] Dubé, *The General Principles for the Reckoning of Time in Canon Law*, The Catholic University of America Canon Law Studies, No. 144 (Washington, D. C.: The Catholic University of America Press, 1941), pp. 71, 82. Hereafter cited as *Reckoning of Time*.

[5] Reiffenstuel, *Ius Canonicum Universum* (5 vols. in 7, Parisiis, 1864–1870), lib. III, tit. XXXI, n. 88; Bachofen, *Compendium Iuris Regularium*, p. 74; Piatus, *Praelectiones Iuris Regularium* (2 vols., Tornaci, 1888), I, 112.

[6] Bastien, *Directoire Canonique* (Maredsous, 1904), n. 532.

[7] *De Religiosis*, II, 133.

[8] Clemens VIII, const., 19 mart. 1603, § 9: ". . . per decennium a professione emissa in Religione perstiterit."—*Fontes*, n. 189.

Code law, the completion of the tenth year was necessary. Authors did not consider whether the ten years had to be spent in the same institute. Indeed, it may be repeated that authors quoted freely from the Constitution *Cum ad regularem,* but rarely added any comments on the requirement.[9]

Another requisite in the Superior of the students set forth in the Constitution was the possession of knowledge sufficient for the exercise of the office. It is most reasonable to demand that a person have sufficient knowledge to exercise properly any office entrusted to him. Such a necessity arises from the very law of nature. It exists even if no positive legislation ever indicated that need. In point are the comments of Gratian, who asserted that ignorance is blameworthy in those appointed to rule,[10] and of Leurenius (1646–1723), who in treating of offices in general stated that an official must possess the knowledge necessary for the proper exercise of an office because it is a demand of nature.[11]

Thus more or less knowledge is required in a Superior according as one office differs from another in its scope and end. The purpose of the office along with positive legislation determines the degree of knowledge requisite in the one exercising any particular authority. The Constitution *Cum ad regularem* declared that the principal work of the Master of novices and of the Superior of the students was the education and training of the novices and the professed students. The novices and the students were to be taught all matters concerning the Rule and Constitutions of their order, the obligation of the vows, the method of prayer, the dangers to the progress of virtue, and the means of attaining sanctity.[12] In other words, the nature of the office, its duties and the instruction to be imparted by its incumbent required both the Master of novices and the Superior of the students to be thoroughly acquainted with the teaching of the masters of the spiritual life, and to understand not only the law in regard to the vows in general, but also the regulations of their

---

[9] Cf. Reiffenstuel, *Ius Canonicum Universum,* lib. III, tit. 31, n. 88; Bachofen, *Compendium Iuris Regularium,* p. 74.

[10] C. 3, 4, D. XXXVIII.

[11] *Forum Beneficiale* (Venetiis, 1742), pars 1, sect. II, cap. I, q. CCXLII.

[12] Clemens VIII, const., 19 mart. 1603, § 9—*Fontes,* n. 189.

own community. The nature of the office was the guide to be followed in deciding the quantity and quality of the knowledge needed by its incumbent to direct others.

Besides the above named qualities, it was also set forth in the Constitution that certain moral qualities should be present in the incumbent of the office. Prudence was held to be needed to direct others to their perfection; charity, mortification, constant prayer, zeal tempered with meekness, gravity with affability, due control of thought and action. All the moral qualities required were to be manifest in order that by good example a practical and living norm of action might be constantly presented to the observation of the students.

Among the older authors Reiffenstuel (1642–1703) was the only one who mentioned these qualities in the Master of novices. Even he merely quoted a long passage from the Constitution *Cum ad regularem,* but added no comment.[13] However, whatever he advocated for the Master of novices was also applicable with reference to the Superior of the students, for the qualities required in the incumbents of both offices were the same.

Article II. The Qualities of the Spiritual Prefect in the Code

A. The Problem

Canon 588, § 2; Praefectus vel Magister spiritus iis qualitatibus praeditus sit oportet, quae in Magistro novitiorum requiruntur ad normam can. 559, §§ 2, 3.

Canon 559—§ 1. Novitiorum institutioni praeficiendus est Magister, qui sit annos natus quinque saltem ac triginta, decem saltem ab annis a prima professione professus, prudentia, caritate, pietate, religionis observantia conspicuus et, si de clericali religione agatur, in sacerdotio constitutus.

§ 2. Si ob novitiorum numerum vel aliam iustam causam expedire visum fuerit, Magistro novitiorum adiungatur socius, eidem immediate subiectus in iis quae ad novitiatus regimen spectant, annos natus saltem triginta, quinque saltem ab annis a prima professione professus, cum ceteris dotibus necessariis et opportunis.

[13] *Ius Canonicum Universum,* lib. III, tit. 31, n. 88.

§ 3. *Uterque ab omnibus officiis oneribusque vacare debet, quae novitiorum curam et regimen impedire valeant.*

Canon 588, § 2, presents one of the most difficult texts for interpretation in the Code of Canon Law. It has been called the "*crux interpretum.*" Writers on this subject always emphasize the difficulty before proceeding to offer a solution.

The problem is this. Canon 588, § 2, states that the Spiritual Prefect of the clerical religious students should have the same qualities as the Master of novices according to canon 559, §§ 2, 3. Yet canon 559, § 2, refers not to the Master of novices, but to the Assistant Master, and canon 559, § 3, imposes a prohibition on the Master and his Assistant, which prohibition forbids their acceptance of incompatible duties and offices. From this inconsistency a difficulty arises, for one canon demands that the Spiritual Prefect have these qualities which the law requires of the Master of novices according as they are found in another canon of the Code. But the canon to which the reference is made enumerates not the qualities of the Master, but those of the Assistant Master.

Faced with this difficulty canonical writers have attempted to offer a solution. The result of this effort points to a division of opinion based on the reaction of authors regarding the reliability of the text. One group maintains that the text contains a typographical error; the other group holds that the text is free from such an error.[14]

Some authors [15] state that there is a real material error in the

[14] "Hinc iam videtur difficultas quae undequaque nos premit. Quia aut dicere mendosam citationem tenebimur, citationem inquam § 2 loco § 1 in qua de qualitatibus Magistri lex fertur; aut convenire Praefecto scholasticorum religiosorum non qualitates Magistri novitiorum, ut textus aliunde expresse dicit, sed potius *Socii* qualitates. Primum nimis audere videtur, alterum contra verba canonis pugnat. Quid ergo?"—Goyeneche, "Consultationes"—*CpR,* I (1920), 141.

[15] Cance, *Le Droit Canonique* (3 vols., Paris: J. Gabalda et Fils, Vol. II, 6. ed., 1930), II, n. 64; Fanfani, *De Iure Religiosorum,* n. 276; Goyeneche, "Consultationes"—*CpR,* I (1920), 141, 142; Canuto, "De regimine domus studiorum in religione clericali exempta ad normam can. 588"—*Apollinaris,* IX (1936), 19–39.

text, namely, that canon 588, § 2, should refer to canon 559, § 1, instead of canon 559, § 2. They say that a mistake was made in the composition of canon 558, § 2, and an incorrect reference resulted. If canon 588, § 2, were made to refer to canon 559, § 1, instead of canon 559, § 2, they contend that all the difficulty of the text would immediately vanish.[16] With this correction it would be clearly evident that the Spiritual Prefect should possess the qualities of the Master of novices, that is, be at least thirty-five years of age, be professed with the vows of religion for at least ten years since his first profession, be endowed with the virtues of prudence, charity and piety, be outstanding in his observance of the Rule and Constitutions, be constituted in the order of priesthood.[17] Goyeneche does not clearly state whether he considers the reference to canon 559, § 3, as also erroneous. He emphasizes the fact that the reference in canon 588, § 2, should be to canon 559, § 1. He is silent as regards the reference to canon 559, § 3.

The more common opinion contends that there is no material error in the text of canon 588, § 2, that its reference is properly assigned, that the legislator meant exactly what is written. But while these authors admit the text to be correct, they divide into two groups in explaining the meaning of the text. Some[18] hold that the Spiritual Prefect should have the same qualities as the Assistant to the Master. The requisite qualities are that the incumbent be at least thirty years of age, that he be at least five years professed from the time of his initial profession, and that he possess the other necessary and useful endowments. Others[19]

[16] "Maxima cum reverentia et quin declarationi, si qua opus sit, Commissionis Pontificiae ad Codicis canones authentice interpretandos praeire intendamus, mendosam citationem credimus ex materiali errore provenientem in transcriptione § 2 loco § 1." Goyeneche, "Consultationes"—*CpR,* I (1920), 141.

[17] Canon 559, § 1.

[18] Coronata, *Institutiones,* I, n. 597; Chelodi, *Ius de Personis,* n. 275, b, footnote 2; Cappello, *Summa Iuris Canonici,* II, n. 619.

[19] Berutti, *Institutiones,* III, n. 100; Oesterle, "De ratione studiorum in religionibus clericalibus"—*CpR,* VI (1925), 305-307; Toso, *Commentaria Minora,* V, 163–164; Vermeersch-Creusen, *Epitome,* I, n. 741; Wernz-Vidal, *Ius Canonicum,* III, n. 332; Sipos, *Enchiridion Iuris Canonici* (3. ed., Pécs: Ex Typographia "Haladas R. T.," 1936), p. 381, footnote 5.

maintain that the Spiritual Prefect must have the qualities of the Master of novices, but in a lesser degree as regards age and the time spent in religious profession. Thus the incumbent of the office would be required to possess the moral qualities of the Master, and the physical qualities of the Assistant to the Master.

B. THE OPINIONS OF THE CANONISTS

The opinion of the authors may be schematically represented as follows:

Canon 588, § 2.	A. Those who affirm the presence of a typographical error.	1. According to this view the qualities should correspond to those of the Master of novices.
	B. Those who deny the presence of any typographical error.	2. According to the first alternative view the qualities should correspond to the Assistant to the Master.
		3. According to the second alternative view the physical qualities should correspond to those of the Assistant, the moral qualities to those of the Master.

The defenders of the respective views are:

A 1. Goyeneche, Fanfani, Cance, Canuto.
B 2. Cappello, Coronata, Chelodi.
B 3. Berutti, Toso, Wernz-Vidal, Vermeersch-Creusen, Oesterle, Sipos, Schaefer.

1. Opinion of Those Who Affirm the Presence of a Typographical Error

The writer will give in detail the arguments of both groups concerning the reliability of the text. He will defend the opinion which holds that there is no typographical error in the text, and that the Spiritual Prefect should possess the physical qualities of the Assistant to the Master and the moral qualities of the Master.

The leading proponent of the typographical error theory is Goyeneche.[20] He defends his opinion with the following arguments. First, the original official edition of the Code of Canon Law was published and promulgated in 1917 in the official commentary of the Holy See, the *Acta Apostolicae Sedis.*[21] In a later edition of the special volume of the *Acta Apostolicae Sedis* as issued towards the end of the same year, 77 emendations were printed, making corrections in the numbers and references of the canons, or changing the spelling and punctuation, or adding words to the text.[22] From the fact that there were some inaccurate constructions in the original work, and from the further fact that the work of composition was a human endeavor, it is not illogical to conclude that there remains a certain possibility for the existence of other uncorrected errors even after the Code began to exercise its finding force in 1918.

But, Goyeneche argues, that which was possible became an actual fact in canon 588, § 2. He concludes that there is in fact an erroneous citation in this canon. Canon 588, § 2, provides that the Spiritual Prefect must possess the same qualities as the Master of novices, not as the Assistant Master. Clearly and unmistakably the reference is made to the Master of novices and his qualifications, and not to the Assistant Master. In the text the legislator directs his primary statement to the qualities of the *Master.* If he then proceeds to add a citation which weakens or even neutralizes the force of his first assertion, it is reasonable to assume that the error is not in the words "*in Magistro novitiorum*" but rather in the misadjusted and misapplied reference. The words "*in Magistro novitiorum*" are plainly written in the text, obvious to all, easy to be condemned if erroneous. On the other hand, the placing of a citation or reference in a canon implies the making of a comparison between canons, the handling

[20] "Consultationes"—*CpR,* I (1920), 141, 142; IX (1928), 117, 118.

[21] *AAS,* IX (1917), Pars II.

[22] *AAS,* IX (1917), Pars II, Appendix, 525–527.

of manuscripts, and even a possible trusting to memory. Though in so important and significant a work as the edition of the Code one could expect a scrupulous checking and rechecking of words and texts and references, nevertheless if an error is to be anticipated, the chances of its happening on account of an erroneous reference are more readily to be admitted than the chances of an actual error in a prominent and important word of the canon. Furthermore, if the legislator meant to write *Assistant Master,* he would have seen the error instantly from even a hurried reading of the canon, for the word *Master* stands out plainly in its capitalized form.

In criticism of the argument, however, it may be said at this point that recourse should never be made to an error in the text, if the text, though unusual and difficult, can be given a probable and reasonable interpretation.

The second argument for the typographical error theory is based on canon 6, 4°, which requires that the previous law be followed whenever a doubt exists in the matter of agreement between the previous and the current law. According to the Constitution *Cum ad regularem* the Spiritual Prefect was to possess the same qualities as the Master of novices, among which were the demands of thirty-five years of age and of ten years of religious profession.[23] If in the current law a doubt remains concerning the requirement of qualities on the part of the Spiritual Prefect even after all the rules of interpretation have been fully applied, then it is necessary to conclude that the law in this regard remains the same today as it existed from the time of Clement VIII to the advent of the current law.

This contention one may answer briefly, without a complete development of the arguments at this point, by stating that the office of the Spiritual Prefect as contemplated in the Code is different from that exercised before the time of the Code.

Goyeneche's third argument is drawn from the practice of clerical religious communities before 1918, which required that the priest in charge of the students be in possession of the same qualities as the Master of novices.[24]

---

[23] Clemens VIII, const., 19 mart. 1603, § 20—*Fontes,* n. 189.

[24] Cited by Goyeneche (*CpR,* I [1920], 142) : *Constitutiones Fratrum S.*

Thus, in summary, the principal arguments for this opinion are: (a) errors are possible in the text because it is an historical fact that they have occurred, and therefore if the text contains an insurmountable difficulty because of an apparent inconsistency between the words and the reference, and if this difficulty immediately vanishes by a change of the references in the text, there is a strong argument that the reference in the text is incorrect; (b) when there is a continuation of a juridic entity in the current law as derived from an antecedent law, and a doubt exists concerning the interpretation of the current law, the interpretation of the antecedent law is to be followed; (c) religious communities before the Code were constant in their interpretation of the law to mean that the Spiritual Prefect should possess the qualities of the Master of novices.

2. *Opinion of Those Who Deny the Presence of Any Typographical Error*

The opinion of the authors who form the second group maintains that the text is a reliable expression of the mind of the legislator, and that the Spiritual Prefect needs to have the qualities of the Master of novices, but in a somewhat lesser degree, that is, more after the manner of the Assistant Master. Oesterle [25] defends this opinion at greater length than do the others. Here the arguments will be given without reference to any writer.

First, there is a strong presumption that the whole Code is an exact expression of the mind of the legislator, that the legislator wrote what he intended, and that the publication of the law is accurate and free from any material error. To fall back on a mechanical defect to explain a difficult text must always be the last adopted resort, defensible only when an insoluble problem still remains in the construction of the canon after the rules of in-

---

Ordinis Praedicatorum (ed. nov. Paris, 1886), Distinct. II, cap. XIV, Decl. I, p. 544 seq.; *Regula et Constitutiones Generales Fratrum Minorum* (Ad Claras Aquas [Quaracchi], 1914), nn. 98, 106; *Regula et Constitutiones Fratrum Discalceatorum Ordinis Beatissimae Virginis Mariae de Monte Carmelo* (Romae, 1906), pars. II, cap. VIII, n. 3.

[25] "De ratione studiorum in religionibus clericalibus"—*CpR,* VI (1925), 305–307.

terpretation have been exhaustingly applied. If the reading of the current law leads to a conclusion which, although sharply differing from the previous law, is nevertheless reasonable according to the text and context, and in harmony with the mind of the legislator, that conclusion is to be accepted despite its departure from the tradition of the past.[26]

Secondly, a strong presumption also exists that not only the whole Code is an accurate expression of the mind of the legislator, but that canon 588, § 2, is the precise reading that the lawmaker intended to be written in the law. In 1917, the same year in which the Code was officially published and promulgated, 77 corrections were made in the original text. In some instances words were added, as in the case of canon 306. Originally the text read: " Missae sacrificium pro populis sibi commissis applicare debent saltem in solemnitatibus Nativitatis Domini, Epiphaniae, *Paschatis, Pentecostes,* sanctissimi Corporis Christi, Immaculatae Conceptionis et Assumptionis Beatae Mariae Virginis, Sancti Ioseph eius sponsi, Sanctorum Apostolorum Petri et Pauli, Omnium Sanctorum, servato praescripto can. 339, §§ seqq." [27] But the corrected version inserted *Ascensionis* between *Paschatis* and *Pentecostes.* Twenty-four emendations of this kind were reported by Cardinal Gasparri to Pope Benedict XV (1914–1922), and the latter ordered these corrections to be made and published in the official commentary of the Holy See.[28]

A second kind of correction was made when a rectification of the spelling, punctuation and references eliminated 53 inaccurate references, omissions and defects. Canon 512, § 3, for instance, originally carried a reference to canons 533–535; the corrected version extended the scope of the reference by including mention also of canon 532. An example of a correction in the punctuation is had in canon 759, § 3, where "*suppleantur; nisi*" was changed to "*suppleantur, nisi.*" All the errors of the second kind —punctuation, misspelling, wrong references—were corrected in the *Acta Apostolicae Sedis,* but no notation is made that they

[26] Canon 18.

[27] *AAS,* IX (1917), Pars II. Italics inserted by the writer.

[28] *AAS,* IX (1917), 557, 589.

were first reported to the Pope for his approval.[29] It appears that they were mechanical errors and could be detected at a glance by means of a comparison of the authentic with the first printed edition.

Canon 588, § 2, contains a correction of the second kind. In the first official edition the canon read: " Praefectus vel Magister spiritus iis qualitatibus praeditus sit oportet, quae in Magistro novitiorum requiruntur ad normam can. 559." [30] In this printing of the Code, canon 588, § 2, did not refer to canon 559, §§ 2, 3, but to canon 559. But in the appendix of the extra volume of the *Acta Apostolicae Sedis* of 1917 the canon was modified so as to present its present reading. By this insertion a distinct change occurred in the significance of the text. However, in the making of such a modification it was necessary for the correctors to study the question thoroughly, to check references, and to weigh well the new terminology. Moreover, when a canon is singled out from hundreds for study and revision, it is to be taken for granted that extreme care will be used for making sure that the new reading will not be faulty. Furthermore, the first reference in canon 588, § 2, a reference to canon 559, was sufficiently clear and would have been understood immediately as applying to the qualities of the Master of novices in canon 559, § 1. A change of reference that would create a so-called insoluble difficulty, apparent even from a hurried reading of the canon by skillful men, would scarcely pass into the Code unobserved by the legislator, when before the correction the insoluble difficulty did not exist. If, then, an alteration was made, it seems far-fetched to say that the correction contains an error and itself needs rectification. Consequently, in the light of the fact that in a small section of a vast legal text there was made a correction which added new significance to the text, a strong presumption is created that the new reference is indeed accurate and not erroneous, even though no mention was made that the revised " *errata,*" among which this reference appeared, were corrected at the command of the Pontiff.

Thirdly, the fact that the new reference in canon 588, § 2, has

[29] *AAS,* IX (197), Pars II, Appendix, 526, 527.

[30] *AAS,* IX (1917), Pars II.

never been corrected strengthens even further the presumption that the present reading is the one intended by the legislator. From the time that "§§ *2, 3*" were affixed to the words "*ad normam can. 559*" as the reference in canon 588, § 2, no subsequent official document has published or adopted any modification of the reference as made in canon 588, § 2. This fact offers added indication of the approbation of the present text, especially when it is known that there is an instance in which the correction of a canon was itself corrected with another modification. Thus in the promulgation of the Code, canon 1252, § 4, read: "Diebus dominicis vel festis de praecepto lex abstinentiae, vel abstinentiae et ieiunii, vel ieiunii tantum cessat, nec pervigilia anticipantur; item cessat Sabbato Sancto post meridiem."[31] Then in the November 1917 issue of the *Acta Apostolicae Sedis* an addition was entered which resulted in the following: "Diebus . . . tantum cessat, *excepto tempore Quadragesimae,* nec pervigilia. . . ."[32] Finally, in the December issue of the *Acta Apostolicae Sedis* of the same year, a *monitum* was given and a correction was made of the second formulation of the wording of canon 1252, § 4. It is this third reading that has become the final one. "Diebus . . . tantum cessat, excepto *festo* tempore Quadragesimae, nec pervigilia. . . ."[33] If someone were to contend that such a mistake offers clear proof that the correction of a text can itself become inaccurate and insufficient, and therefore remain subject to further correction, he should also be ready to admit that the same case furnishes an argument that the proper authorities did revise the earlier correction when the need of further correction was indicated. Consequently, in view of the fact that the present reference in canon 588, § 2, is itself a correction of another reference, but was never altered in any way, the present text must stand as the precise expression of the mind of the legislator, unless the Holy See determines otherwise in the future.

Fourthly, the interpretation adopted by the commentator must

[31] *AAS,* IX (1917), Pars II.

[32] Secretaria Status, 17 oct. 1917—*AAS,* IX (1917), 557. Italics in the quoted correction of the text are inserted by the writer.

[33] *AAS,* IX (1917), 589. Italics inserted in the text by the writer.

accept the canon for what it is and thus attempt to give it meaning. In the original text of canon 588, § 2, the reference was made to canon 559. Anyone reading and interpreting the two canons would have readily concluded that the legislator had in mind canon 559, § 1, where the qualities of the Master of novices are stated. But the reference in canon 588, § 2, was changed to canon 559, §§ 2, 3, and immediately canon 588, § 2, became an unusual canon. It provides that the Spiritual Prefect must have the qualities of the Master of novices according to canon 559, §§ 2, 3, yet, strange to say, neither § 2 nor § 3 of canon 559 directly concerns the qualities of the Master of novices. In § 2 the qualities of the Assistant Master of novices are enumerated, while in § 3 there is nothing stated whatsoever about the qualities of anybody. Rather, in this last section of canon 559 there is a prohibition against extraneous assignments that might interfere with the work of the Master of novices and his Assistant. This section of the canon is, therefore, as difficult to harmonize with canon 588, § 2, as is the reference to the Assistant. But since this difficulty arose only after a correction was made in the text, it seems that a strong presumption has been thus created that the text is the exact expression of the mind of the legislator, and hence it has become necessary to proceed with a conciliatory interpretation.

According to canon 588, § 2, there should be found in the Spiritual Prefect the same general qualities as in the Master, but in the modified form determined by canon 559, § 2, where the qualities of the Assistant are enumerated. The qualities called for by canon 559, § 1, in its direct application to the Master turn about the considerations of age, of length of religious profession, of ordination to the priesthood, and of certain moral endowments of character. Those enumerated in canon 559, § 2, as required for the Assistant revolve around the factors of age, of length of religious profession, and of other necessary and useful qualities. An age of thirty-five years and a term of ten years of religious profession are assigned as requisites for the Master; an age of thirty years and a term of five years of religious profession are indicated for the Assistant. Therefore, the Spiritual Prefect must meet the *requirements* regarding age and length of profession as called for in both Master and Assistant, but the qualities need be possessed only to that *degree* in which they are called for in the Assistant, namely, an age of thirty years and a term of five years of religious profession. As for the other qualifications, the statement of canon 559, § 2, is very general. It implies simply that other necessary and useful qualities are needed in the Assistant. But canon 588, § 2, already has stated that the qualities of the Spiritual Prefect should be the same as those of the Master, leaving room only for the implied exception of the modifications introduced by canon 559, § 2, which treats of the Assistant. Therefore, since there are no modifications in canon 559, § 2, besides those which touch considerations of the requisite age and the required length of religious profession, the other necessary and useful qualities demanded of the Spiritual Prefect are simply those which are required of the Master, namely, prudence, charity, piety, exemplary observance of the ideal of the religious life, and ordination to the priesthood.[34]

Thus the meaning of canon 588, § 2, becomes the following: the Spiritual Prefect should have the same qualities as the Master of novices, as adapted to any of the modifications introduced by canon 559, § 2; and just as the Master and his Assistant are forbidden to exercise any office or to assume any burdens incompatible with their primary assignment, so too the Spiritual Prefect is prohibited from assuming any duties which will interfere with his spiritual direction of the clerical professed students.

Fifthly, the Sacred Congregation for Religious, after examining the corrected Rules and Constitutions of clerical religious orders and congregations, has approved some Rules and Constitutions which do not require that the Spiritual Prefect be endowed with all the qualities which by common law are required of the Master of novices.[35]

---

[34] "Non proprie de Magistro, sed de *socio* Magistri novitiorum agitur in can. 559, § 2; quia tamen ibidem decernitur ut Socius Magistri novitiorum sit 'annos natus saltem triginta, quinque saltem ab annis a prima professione professus, *cum ceteris dotibus necessariis et opportunis*,' ex praescripto can. 588, § 2 certo scimus huiusmodi dotes in Magistro spiritus eas esse debere quae in can. 559, § 1 requiri dicuntur in Magistro novitiorum."—Berutti, *Institutiones,* III, n. 100.

[35] Cf. *Constitutiones Piae Societatis Missionum* (Ratisbonae: Pustet, post

In summarizing the foregoing arguments in defense of the opinion that the Spiritual Prefect should have the same qualities as the Master of novices, barring only the considerations of personal age and of the length of religious profession, one may restate the foregoing reasons as follows: (a) a presumption exists that all the canons in the Code are correctly formulated in their intent to give expression to the mind of the legislator; (b) there is a further presumption that the more minutely specified reference as inserted in canon 588, § 2, is correct, for the added mention of §§ 2, 3, in relation to canon 559 was inserted into the Code after the official edition had been published; (c) no subsequent revision of the previous correction was ever made; (d) the wording of canon 588, § 2, fully allows the interpretation which contends that the Spiritual Prefect should have the qualities of the Master of novices, with proper allowance being made for the modifications set forth in canon 559, § 2; (e) some religious Constitutions require an age of but thirty years and a time of but five years of religious profession for the Spiritual Prefect. Extrinsic authority for this interpretation is derived from the support of such writers as Berutti, Toso, Wernz-Vidal, Vermeersch-Creusen, Oesterle, Sipos, Schaefer.[86]

---

annum 1922), nn. 170, 171. Although this society is constituted of members living in common without public vows, nevertheless the prescriptions of canon 587, 588, 591, are imposed upon the society as laws to be followed. The practice whereby clerical communities which are not strictly religious communities nevertheless follow the law which is enacted for religious institutes in regard to houses of study is altogether in conformity with the provision which canon 678 invokes in favor of special prescriptions emanating from the Holy See. An age of thirty years and a term of five years of pledged affiliation with the community are the requirements of the Constitutions. Cf. also *The Rule and General Constitutions of the Friars Minor* (Paterson, N. J.: St. Anthony Guild Press, 1936), n. 99. An age of thirty years is set as the requirement. The Constitutions are silent in regard to the required number of years of religious profession.

[86] Berutti, *Institutiones,* III, n. 100; Toso, *Commentaria Minora,* V, 163–164; Wernz-Vidal, *Ius Canonicum,* III, n. 332; Vermeersch-Creusen, *Epitome,* I, n. 741; Oesterle, "De ratione studiorum in religionibus clericalibus"—*CpR,* VI (1925), 305–307; Sipos, *Enchiridion,* p. 381, footnote 5; Schaefer, *De Religiosis,* p. 634.

3. Objections

Canuto,[37] instituting a comparison between the text of the Constitution of Clement VIII and the wording of the present law in canon 588, § 2, concludes from the great similarity between the two passages that the law of canon 588, § 2, should be explained according to interpretational norm sanctioned by canon 6, 2°.[38] The texts of the Constitution of Clement VIII and of canon 588, § 2, read as follows:

Constitution of Clement VIII	". . . et [studentes] debebunt literarum studiis operam navare, sub directione, ac regimine Superioris, qui eas qualitates habeat, quibus Novitiorum Magistrum praeditum esse oportere dictum est."
Canon 588, § 2.	"Praefectus vel Magister spiritus iis qualitatibus praeditus sit oportet, quae in Magistro novitiorum requiruntur ad normam can. 559, §§ 2, 3."

In reply to this contention it may be readily admitted that there is a great similarity between the wording in the old and the new law, but there is also a difference created by reason of the introduction of a modification. The first official reading of the text of the Code in its official promulgation in the *Acta Apostolicae Sedis* was in complete agreement with the text in the old law. But a correction was made in the text, and thereby a new idea was added to the canon. Consequently, the canon must be explained in the light of the interpretational norm enacted in canon 6, 3°, and not according to the norm sanctioned in canon 6, 2°.[39]

Again it is objected: Why did not the legislator use the word "socius" instead of "Magister" in canon 588, § 2, if he in-

---

[37] "De regimine domus studiorum in religione clericali exempta ad normam can. 588"—*Apollinaris*, IX (1936), 19–39.

[38] "Canones qui ius vetus ex integro referunt, ex veteris iuris auctoritate, atque ideo ex receptis apud probatos auctores interpretationibus, sunt aestimandi."

[39] Canon 6, 3°: "Canones qui ex parte tantum cum veteri iure congruunt, qua congruunt, ex iure antiquo aestimandi sunt; qua discrepant, sunt ex sua ipsorum sententia diiudicandi."

tended that the Spiritual Prefect should possess the qualities of the Assistant Master?

It is the opinion defended in this work that the legislator did not intend the Spiritual Prefect to have the same qualities as the Assistant Master, for in such an instance he would have used the word "socius." Neither did he intend that the qualities coincide with those of the Master; otherwise the modifications introduced in canon 588, § 2, by the reference to canon 559, §§ 2, 3, would not have been incorporated into the text. Hence, canon 588, § 2, although an unusual construction, must be considered both in its words and in its reference. To emphasize one of these items to the exclusion of the other will lead to a conclusion which can be justified only by postulating an error in the text.

Another objection arises from the consideration of the relative dignity of the office of the Spiritual Prefect. Canuto [40] states that the dignity of the office of the Spiritual Prefect is not only not inferior to that of the Master of novices, but in a sense is even more noble and of greater moment, inasmuch as clerical students are placed under the guidance of a Spiritual Prefect in preparation for the exalted goal of sacred orders.

In reply one may state that in the novitiate of clerical religious institutes the Master of novices begins the training of the novice for the latter's profession in a community which performs the sacerdotal works of the ministry. These works of the ministry constitute part of the purpose for which the institute was erected. Consequently the spiritual training for these duties should begin in the novitiate where the Master of novices can fruitfully warn, advise, encourage and instill ideals in the novices during the period in which they are the most receptive for direction and instruction. Since the clerical institute expects its novices to proceed to the reception of sacred orders and to perform the works of sacred orders, and since the novice makes profession in order to proceed to the priestly work which is intimately bound up with the purpose of the institute, then from the very beginning of the novitiate the novice should be directed in the acquisition

[40] "De regimine domus studiorum in religione clericali exempta ad normam can. 588"—*Apollinaris*, IX (1936), 31.

of the virtues and the extirpation of the vices which are especially needed to fulfill the obligation of his religious profession both outside the monastery in the works of the ministry as well as within the confines of the religious house.

The Spiritual Prefect continues the formation of the clerical students on their departure from the novitiate. But he does not have the supervision of their external discipline. He has charge of the *spiritual life* of the clerics. He is concerned with the *soul's* advancement. He is a *Magister* SPIRITUS. He advances the progress of all in the *religious* life by instructions, exhortations and admonitions, not by precepts. He has not been given any authority in the external forum by the common law. He does not possess as much authority, as much responsibility, as the Master who has both the spiritual formation of the novices and the discipline of the novitiate entrusted to him.[41] Consequently there is not the same need for him to be endowed with precisely the same qualities as the Master of novices.[42]

After a consideration of the various defended opinions and of the arguments offered in support of them, it is the conclusion of the writer that the more probable opinion is the one which maintains that the Spiritual Prefect should possess the physical qualities of the Assistant Master, that is, those looking to the requirements of age and the length of religious profession, but the moral qualities of the Master, as demanded in the law of canon 559, § 1. Goyeneche, the chief antagonist of this opinion, admits it to be solidly probable in view of the representative list of authors who defend it, but on the grounds of intrinsic evidence regards it to be less probable than his own opinion. Accordingly, he concludes that those who appoint the Spiritual Prefect may choose him from candidates who are but thirty years old.[43]

The opinion of Goyeneche, which maintains that the text of

---

[41] Canons 561; 562; 565.

[42] This argumentation was followed in view of the fact that Canuto himself defends the position which denies the Spiritual Prefect any and all authority in the external forum as derivable from his office. Canuto deals with this matter in his article "De regimine domus studiorum in religione clericali ad normam can. 588"—*Apollinaris,* IX (1936), 19–39.

[43] "Consultationes"—*CpR,* IX (1928), 118.

canon 588, § 2, contains a typographical error, and that the Spiritual Prefect should possess the qualities of the Master, seems to have some probability in the light of the intrinsic evidence derivable from the reasons adduced, and in consequence of the extrinsic authority arising from the support which various authors accord to that opinion.[44] But since that opinion sets up added restrictions in a matter which otherwise leaves free action in the exercise of rights, it reflects an interpretation which cannot be incontestably urged in law, and therefore cannot be strictly demanded in fact.

The third opinion, which holds that the text of canon 588, § 2, is an accurate statement of the mind of the lawgiver and thereupon concludes that the Spiritual Prefect must indeed be endowed with all the qualities postulated for the Assistant Master, but is also sufficiently endowed if he possesses the sole qualities which the law demands, seems to enjoy little if any probability as derivable from intrinsic evidence. The text of canon 588, § 2, does not contain the word "*socius.*" If the legislator had intended to see this word placed in the text of canon 588, its erroneous omission would have been obvious to him at a glance, for the plainly different word "*Magister*" stands in its supposed place in the text. Confronted with this objection, this group of authors presents its chief argument thus: the Assistant may in a wide sense be called the Master of novices. The rightfulness of this assumption is guaranteed by the fact that the specific numerical reference as made in canon 588, § 2, points to the Assistant, and not to the Master.[45] However it appears that the authors resorted to this strained interpretation as the only alternative they saw open to preserve the consistency of the text. Whatever probability the opinion of these authors may have must apparently attach to whatever authority they possess as authors. Their internal argument compels little if any conviction.

[44] Goyeneche, "Consultationes"—*CpR,* I (1920), 141, 143; Fanfani, *De Iure Religiosorum,* n. 276; Canuto, "De regimine domus studiorum in religione clericali ad normam can. 588"—*Apollinaris,* IX (1936), 19-39; Cance, *Le Droit Canonique,* II, n. 64.

[45] Cappello, *Summa Iuris Canonici,* II, n. 619; Chelodi, *Ius de Personis,* n. 275; Coronata, *Institutiones,* I, n. 598; Beste, *Introductio in Codicem* (2. ed., Collegeville, Minn.: St. John's Abbey Press, 1944), p. 400.

If, notwithstanding the provisions of canon 588, the Rule of a religious institute states that the Spiritual Prefect must be endowed with the same qualities as the Master of novices, the prescriptions of the Rule must be followed. If the Rule states that the Spiritual Prefect must possess the qualities of the Master of novices according to the prescription of canon 588, § 2, or according to the rule of canon 559, §§ 2, 3, then all the qualities which are postulated for the Master must also be considered as demanded of the Spiritual Prefect, with the exception of the requirements which look to the age of the incumbent or to the length of his religious profession. In these two matters it suffices that the prospective Spiritual Prefect have the length of years and of religious profession which the law demands in the case of a prospective Assistant Master. This is to say, then, that for his appointment the Spiritual Prefect must be a person who is thirty years old and who has spent at least five years in his religious profession.

Article III. The Specific Qualities of the Spiritual Prefect

As to the physical qualities, the Spiritual Prefect must have the same qualities as the Assistant Master of novices; as to the other qualities, he is required to have the same endowments as the Master. Physical qualities may be defined as those which can be determined in an exact degree by the principles of canon law. The moral qualities are the virtues existing in a person in a greater or lesser degree. For the sake of clarity it should here be stated that ordination to the priesthood will be considered not along with the physical qualities, but along with the moral ones.

A. Age

Although the writer holds the opinion that the Spiritual Prefect is required to have merely the same age as the Assistant Master, nevertheless, the opinion which asserts that the age of the Master of novices constitutes the norm also for that of the Spiritual Prefect will also be taken into account at this point for the sake of thoroughness and particularly inasmuch as some religious institutes in their Constitutions demand precisely the same qualities in every respect for the Spiritual Prefect and for the Master of novices. If the qualifications which are established for the Master serve as the model to be followed in a given institute, the age required for the Spiritual Prefect is thirty-five completed years; if the age of the Assistant constitutes the norm, only thirty completed years are necessary. This is clear from the text of the law which states as requisite qualities in the Master of novices and in his Assistant that the former be "annos natus quinque saltem ac triginta" and the latter "annos natus saltem triginta."[46]

From the fact that the Code makes use of the cardinal number along with the word "*saltem,*" it is clear that the final year in a series of years must be completed and not merely begun.[47] The Spiritual Prefect must, therefore, have completed his thirty-fifth or thirtieth year according as the age established for the Master of novices or that required in the Assistant constitutes the norm to be followed. For determining the exact day and hour, canon 34, § 3, 3°, gives the rule. The *terminus a quo,* implicitly assigned by the birth, ordinarily does not coincide with midnight of the first day. Consequently the first day is not counted, and the completion of the thirty-fifth or the thirtieth year respectively is reached on the day after these anniversaries. If the time of birth coincided with the very beginning of the day, the respective final years are completed on the thirty-fifth or the thirtieth anniversary respectively.[48]

Could a priest be licitly appointed to this office if at the time of the appointment he failed by a very brief space of time to have the required age? First, this problem will be considered as present in a situation in which the Superior has to make a selection from five or six suitable candidates. It must be remembered that the quality of age is one that can be mathematically determined by the juridical principles governing the computation of time. The required duration or lapse of time must be physically complete. In some instances this requirement is set even as an

---

[46] Canon 559, §§ 1, 2.

[47] Dubé, *Reckoning of Time,* p. 253.

[48] Canon 34, § 3, 2°.

essential condition for the validity of an act which is made contingent on the element of time in its performance.[49]

The law in regard to the age of the Spiritual Prefect requires a mathematically exact computation of time, so that the requisite final year must be completed to the letter. Thus, unless the required age is attained, the appointment is illicitly made. Suppose, however, the case wherein the quarterly meeting of the Council in making appointments in August found that the candidate would not be thirty years old until September. In this situation the selection of the candidate could be made in August with the provision that the appointment was not to be effective until September. If, however, the Spiritual Prefect was appointed while below the required age, the appointment, though illicit, would be valid inasmuch as there is no invalidating clause in the law which sets the requirement of age.[50]

If it is desired to appoint one who lacks the requisite age, there must be adequate grounds for the petition which would seek a dispensation from the Holy See. If five or six men are available, it seems that the Superior is bound to follow the exact prescription of the law in making the appointment. Yet if one under the required age had special qualifications not possessed by the remaining candidates, the Superior could laudably seek a dispensation.

The second situation to be reckoned with is that in which few suitable religious for the office of Spiritual Prefect are available because of the small number of religious in the institute, or because of the large number of suitable religious already employed in other important work, and the Superior must choose from a very limited number of candidates, for example, from two or three. May he select a religious under thirty years of age if the latter possesses the other necessary qualifications? In this case one may follow the opinion of Vermeersch,[51] who says that the word "oportet" in canon 588, § 2, is not so absolute in its intent as to demand the strict fulfillment of its requirements in every circumstance, but only when there is a representative number of

---

[49] Canons 504, 555, § 1, 1o.

[50] Canons 588, § 2; 12; 153, § 3.

[51] *Epitome,* I, n. 741; cf. also *infra,* pp. 82–84.

candidates from which a selection can be made. Thus, according to that view, a Superior could choose for the office of Spiritual Prefect a religious who is but twenty-eight years of age if the latter is otherwise qualified and the number of candidates is very small. If the age requirement for the Spiritual Prefect is thirty-five years of age according to the Constitutions, the prescript must be just as exactly followed as if the age were set at thirty years, but the view of Vermeersch would seem applicable also in this case.

Must a priest have the required age and the other necessary qualities if he be delegated for a very short time to supply the place of an absent Spiritual Prefect? An example of this kind could occur in the case in which some other priest is appointed to give two or three conferences to the students. In such an instance the assignment is a mere act of delegation to supply the place of another for an act or an occasion. It does not constitute the delegated person the incumbent of the office. In such a case the requirements need not be fulfilled to the exact letter, for the religious is not appointed to an office, but simply performs an act of the office on one or the other occasion.

B. LENGTH OF RELIGIOUS PROFESSION

The principles employed for computing the age required in the Spiritual Prefect are also to be followed in determining the date of expiration of the five and ten years of religious profession as required in the incumbent of this office. Whether it be ten complete years or five complete years of religious profession which the common law or the Constitutions require, the requisite final year ends on the day after the tenth or the fifth anniversaries according to canon 34, § 3, 3°, that is, in the usual case, inasmuch as the act of religious profession is usually made in the morning or in the afternoon, and not at the midnight hour. The *terminus a quo* is the day of the first profession as made upon the completion of a valid novitiate.

The law does not state that the five or ten requisite years of profession must be spent in the *same* religious institute, as it does for the case of the election of religious Superiors.[52] Creusen

[52] Cf. 504; 559, §§ 1, 2.

therefore contends that the law should be interpreted strictly, and that an aggregate of ten years or five years of religious profession is sufficient to qualify the candidate, although the total number of years is made up of time which the religious spend in two or more religious communities.[53] Besides basing his argument on the wording of canon 559, §§ 1, 2, Creusen, to forestall an anticipated objection arising from the purpose of the law, offers the added remark that a religious coming from another institute may acquire in a short space of time the spirit of the new institute. He acknowledges that the case of an appointment to the office following shortly after the transfer is indeed an exceptional one, but by no means a purely imaginary case.[54]

Berutti admits that the Code does not say that the ten or five years of profession which are required as a qualification for this office must be spent in the same institute. But he maintains that such was the pre-Code law, which in regard to other matters affecting the novitiate has remained unchanged. He also says that the purpose of the law would be frustrated if the required years could be counted as a total of the time spent under vows in two or more institutes. For, if this were admitted in principle, it could happen that a religious would be made a Master of novices even immediately after his profession, inasmuch as he could have spent five or ten years in religious profession in view of a previous profession in other institutes.[55]

This latter argument is one of a practical nature, but even as such it seems far-fetched and lacking in conviction. In making a choice the electors would have to consider the moral qualities of the candidate, his ability to understand the Constitutions and to impart the knowledge of them to others, his prudence in acting, his zeal for religious discipline. Those making the selection would be obliged to be especially cautious in regard to a person who had been transferred from one institute to another. They would normally feel compelled to wait for some years before proceeding to such an appointment, until the religious had given sufficient

[53] Creusen-Ellis-Garesché, *Religious Men and Women in the Code* (4. ed., Milwaukee: Bruce, 1940), n. 204.

[54] *Religious Men and Women in the Code,* n. 204.

[55] Berutti, *Institutiones,* III, n. 79.

signs of his competency. It seems to the writer that the candidate who has been professed for a total of five years, whether the time is made up in one or more institutes, as long only as all the other necessary conditions are verified, can be licitly chosen as the Spiritual Prefect.

C. MORAL QUALITIES

Besides the above discussed requisites the law also demands that the Spiritual Prefect be endowed with certain spiritual qualities. The Code determines what these virtues are. It does not state how or when they should be acquired.

Prudence, charity, piety and zeal for religious observance constitute the requirements of the Spiritual Prefect as specified by the Code. They are appropriate requirements in one who is to lead others to perfection both by word and example. Charity, as mentioned in the canon, is the theological virtue, while prudence is the cardinal or moral virtue. Piety, however, as it appears in this text, refers rather to a holy manner of life, an accumulation of virtues, than to the virtue of piety in its strict theological meaning. Piety, as a part of the virtue of justice, is a special virtue by which submission and reverence are shown to parents and to one's country.[56] This virtue is exercised in the fulfillment of the duties of children toward their parents, and of subjects toward their superiors, although both parents and superiors are bound by reciprocal duties toward their children and their subjects respectively.

In the Clementine law,[57] piety as a virtue was not enumerated among those which were required of the Master of novices and the Spiritual Prefect. In fact, the word piety is not found in the text of that Constitution. Nevertheless, the law did require that the Master and his Assistant be faithful to mental prayer, constant in mortifications and conspicuous for the practice of many other virtues, as for example zeal tempered with meekness, or

[56] Cf. Merkelbach, *Summa Theologiae Moralis ad Mentem D. Thomae et ad Normam Iuris Canonici* (3 vols., Vol. II, *De Virtutibus Moralibus*), 3. ed., Parisiis: Desclée de Brouwer et Soc., 1938), II, n. 836. Hereafter cited as *Summa Theologiae Moralis.*

[57] Const., "*Cum ad regularem,*" 19 mart. 1603, §§ 9, 20—*Fontes,* n. 189.

seriousness tempered with affability. Consequently, since these virtues are not specifically mentioned in the present law, and since piety was not explicitly required in the pre-Code law, it appears that the word piety in the present law is a substitution for the long list of virtues enumerated in the earlier law, and refers rather to an accumulation of virtues, a holy manner of life, than to the virtue of piety in its strict theological meaning. Charity and prudence, on the other hand, were also specifically enumerated in the Clementine law as they are now recounted in the Code. Finally, there is the requirement of ordination to the priesthood. This requirement must be met whenever there is question of the appointment of a Spiritual Prefect in a clerical religious institute. The law obliges in all clerical religious institutes, exempt and non-exempt alike.

Article IV. The Force of the Word "Oportet"

The Spiritual Prefect should possess the following qualities: the age of at least thirty years; a religious profession of at least five years' duration; the possession of the order of the priesthood; prudence, charity, piety, and zeal for the observance of the religious life and discipline. In stating the necessity of these qualities, the legislator uses the word "*oportet.*" What is the force of this word? Does it mean that it is *fitting* for the man appointed to the office of Spiritual Prefect to possess the qualities named? Or does it mean that it is *necessary* that he be so equipped? In other words, does canon 588, § 2, through the use of the word "*oportet*" create a strict obligation, or does it merely suggest a counsel?

It must be replied that the word "*oportet*" in this canon imposes a strict obligation. This is apparent (a) from the intention of the legislator in framing the Code of Canon Law; (b) from the text and context of canon 588, § 2; and (c) from a consideration of the force of the word "*oportet*" as it occurs generally in other canons in the Code.

First, in the Apostolic Constitution *Providentissima Mater Ecclesia* of Benedict XV, by means of which the Code of Canon Law was promulgated, the Supreme Pontiff decreed and ordered that the newly codified work should enjoy the force of law for the whole church.

> "Itaque, invocato divinae gratiae auxilio, Beatorum Petri et Pauli Apostolorum auctoritate confisi, motu proprio, certa scientia atque Apostolicae, qua aucti sumus, potestatis plenitudine, Constitutione hac Nostra, quam volumus perpetuo valituram, praesentem Codicem, sic ut digestus est, *promulgamus, vim legis posthac habere pro universa Ecclesia decernimus, iubemus,* vestraeque tradimus custodiae ac vigilantiae servandum." [58]

Since the legislator has given to the Code the force of law, and not merely the force of an instruction, or of an exhortation or counsel, it must be conclusively presumed that each canon places an obligation on the subject unless the terminology in a particular canon indicates that the lawmaker in this or that instance has decided to publish a counsel or a desire.

When a legislator establishes and promulgates a Code, ordinarily he gives laws, commands. If he counsels in some particular matter, it is to be expected that he will use words which readily reveal his intention to his subjects. The presumption, then, exists that all the canons impose an obligation, unless the words of a particular canon clearly manifest the contrary.

The Code offers many examples in which the lawmaker merely offers counsel, and does not impose a strict obligation, namely, when he states the reasonableness, appropriateness or suitableness of an indicated manner of acting without commanding the subjects to obey.[59] Canon 399, § 1, for instance, enumerates the qualities requisite in the canon theologian and the canon penitentiary in the cathedral chapter. Concerning the age of the latter the canon states that it is *expedient* that he have attained his thirtieth completed year. Another expression which also is of less force than the term "*oportet*" is the word "*decet.*" It occurs in the canons on baptism and confirmation.[60] Canon 772

---

[58] *AAS,* XII (1917), Pars II, 8. Also found in all editions of the Code of Canon Law.

[59] E. g., canons 399, § 1; 530, § 2; 772; 790; 864, § 2; 866, § 2; 1262, § 1; 1345; 1379, § 2; 1380.

[60] Canons 772; 790.

states that it is *becoming* that the solemn baptism of adults be administered on the vigils of Easter and Pentecost, and canon 790 asserts that it is *becoming* that the sacrament of confirmation be confirmed during the week of Pentecost. In still other places the law uses such expressions as "*optandum*," "*suadendum est.*"[61]

From a consideration of these milder expressions as found in the law it is evident that the legislator sometimes issues a counsel instead of a command. However, when he does counsel, he uses words which clearly manifest his intention. Otherwise it is conclusively taken for granted that every canon imposes an obligation.

Secondly, the text in Canon 588, § 2, has the force of an imperative construction. The word "*oportet*" does not stand alone but is preceded by "*praeditus sit.*" In an imperative construction the use of the word "*sit*" points to the issuing of a command. Standing outside a code of law this expression would indicate a command without necessarily denoting any moral necessity to follow the command, but employed by the legislator it imposes an order to be obeyed. "*Oportet*" emphasizes the compulsory nature of the command. It does not take away or weaken the command of the legislator as already indicated with the expression "*sit,*" but determines more precisely the degree to which the subject is bound to obey. To judge the degree of compulsion implied in the word "*oportet,*" it is necessary to consult parallel places in the Code to discover how the legislator uses the construction of "*oportet*" with the subjunctive.

This construction is found in canon 377, § 1.[62] Cocchi interprets it to mean "*debet.*"[63] A very clear example of the use of "*oportet*" with the subjunctive as imposing an obligation is the provision of canon 1459, § 2, in which occur the words ". . . accedat oportet Ordinarii consensus. . . ." Here the subjunctive is used with "*oportet,*" yet it is perfectly evident that the canon commands, under pain of invalidity, that if there are several independent patrons and they make an agreement for themselves and their successors to exercise the right of presentation in

---

[61] E. g., canons 864, § 2; 866, § 2; 1262, § 1; 1379, § 2; 1380.

[62] "Archivum clausum sit oportet et nemini illud ingredi liceat sine Episcopi aut Vicarii Generalis et cancellarii licentia."

[63] *Commentarium* (Vol. III, 4. ed., 1940), III, n. 289.

rotation, the written permission of the Ordinary must be obtained. In this canon a definite obligation is imposed, and to such an extent that a violation of the canon causes invalidity in the act of agreement of the patrons. Again, in canon 588, § 2, under a construction similar to that of canon 1459, § 2, a definite obligation is also imposed.

Thirdly, the word "*oportet*" occurs frequently throughout the Code.[64] In all the cases in which it is employed the law enacts an obligation or considers a need for action. Sometimes it is required by the use of the word that the conditions in the law must be fulfilled in order that certain actions be valid. Thus canons 765 and 795 state the conditions necessary that sponsors in baptism and confirmation may act validly, and canon 573 stresses one of the conditions for valid profession of vows in a religious community. In some other cases the law must be fulfilled for the lawfulness of the act. Canons 766 and 796 enumerate the conditions required that sponsors may licitly act in baptism and confirmation while canon 111 requires all clerics to be assigned to some diocese or affiliated with some religious institute. From a consideration, therefore, of the manner in which the word "*oportet*" is used in these and other canons of the Code, the conclusion must be reached that the word is used not to express a counsel, but to impose an obligation.

Vermeersch injects a difficulty into the question by saying that the word "*oportet*" of itself is stronger than "*decet,*" but not as forceful as "*necesse est.*" According to him, it is too much to say that it is absolutely necessary in every circumstance that the qualities mentioned in canon 588, § 2, be present in the Spiritual Prefect, while it is not enough to say that it is merely becoming or fitting that they be verified. According to this author, the exact meaning of "*oportet*" falls between these two extremes and imposes an obligation on the Superior to choose a man with the required qualities, provided that there is an abundance of suitable candidates from which to choose.[65] Finally, he asserts that there

---

[64] Canons 41; 111; 180; 247, § 4; 765; 766; 795; 796; 1324; 1347, § 1; 1471; 1474; 1585, § 1.

[65] *Epitome,* I, n. 741.

is no reason for departing from the natural signification of the word "*oportet*" as it occurs in canon 588, § 2.

Oesterle[66] correctly answers this argument by pointing out that, in any attempt to decide the force of the term "*oportet*" in the Code, it is of paramount importance to investigate the manner in which the word is employed by the legislator, since understanding a term according to its proper signification requires that the juridic meaning be taken into account.[67] In using this word in the Code the legislator undoubtedly has given it the force of a strict obligation. It may also be pointed out here that while "*necesse est*" of itself is stronger than "*oportet*," nevertheless in those canons which impose an obligation, indeed in which validity is sometimes under consideration, the lawmaker chooses the word "*oportet*" in many instances.[68] The expression "*necesse est*" does indeed occur in the Code. Now since the legislator does make use of it, one could feel inclined to think that this is the clause most suitable for use in those instances in which absolute necessity needs to be stressed, as when validity is made to depend on the fulfillment of the law. But "*oportet*" instead is employed in the text in those very instances. This fact offers strong proof that the legislator wished to give the meaning of a strict obligation to the term.

Some authors[69] merely restate the words of canon 588, § 2, without commenting on the force of the word "*oportet*." Goyeneche[70] and Oesterle[71] insist on the strict obligation which is signified by the term. Cocchi[72] follows the same interpretation. He uses the word "*debet*" to give expression to the meaning of the term "*oportet*" by way of synonymous rendering.

Vermeersch[73] cites a case in which the Sacred Congregation

---

66 "De ratione studiorum in religionibus clericalibus"—*CpR,* VI (1925), 304.

67 Vermeersch-Creusen, *Epitome,* I, n. 123.

68 E. g., canons 111; 765; 766; 795; 796; 1459, § 2.

69 Berutti, *Institutiones,* III, n. 100; Fanfani, *De Iure Religiosorum,* n. 276.

70 "Consultationes"—*CpR,* I (1920), 142–144.

71 "De ratione studiorum in religionibus clericalibus"—*CpR,* VI (1925), 304.

72 *Commentarium,* IV, n. 87.

73 *Epitome,* I, n. 741.

of Religious was asked for a dispensation to allow a priest under thirty years of age to assume the office of Spiritual Prefect. The answer of the Sacred Congregation was: " Superior utatur iure suo." The response was private, and therefore is not an authentic interpretation binding on all.[74] Nevertheless, it throws some light on the doctrinal interpretation. This private decision of the Sacred Congregation was given in 1924.

Only a few authors had written on this question prior to the year 1924, and a real doubt of law existed at that time, as apparently it does also today, concerning the meaning of the word, and the Superior was given freedom to utilize the milder opinion.[75] Though it seems to the writer that the opinion which supports the contention that the concept of a strict obligation is inherent in the term " oportet " is intrinsically the more probable one, yet the other opinion is also probable, by reason of the extrinsic authority which vouches for it, and consequently may be followed in practice. Thus the Superior may choose one who does not possess the required qualities in their fulness, if there is a dearth of candidates from which to choose.

[74] Canon 17, § 3.

[75] Canon 15.

CHAPTER VII

THE CONFESSION OF SINS AND THE MANIFESTATION OF CONSCIENCE

Both the confession of sins and the manifestation of conscience concern the internal life of an individual. Both are means for advancing the progress of his spiritual life. In both cases the subject manifests the internal activities of his soul to another. But the purpose for which each is made differs. The subject makes a manifestation of conscience in order to obtain spiritual direction from an experienced spiritual leader. He confesses his sins in order to have them forgiven. Manifestation of conscience covers a wider field than confession of sins. It deals not only with spiritual defects, but also virtues, temptations and irregular inclinations.

The priest who receives the confession and manifestation of conscience is concerned in both cases with the salvation of the soul. As a confessor he acts as a judge, a teacher, a spiritual physician and a father.[1] But he exercises these rôles inasmuch as they are needed for the valid and licit administration of the sacrament of Penance, namely, for disposing the penitent to obtain the forgiveness of sins or to safeguard the preservation of his state of grace.[2] His action is the action of a minister of the sacrament of Penance, a ministerial action that produces its effects chiefly *ex opere operato,* that is, through the fact that the sacrament has been validly administered and worthily received.

On the other hand, in acting as a spiritual director, the priest learns the state of the soul through a manifestation of conscience in order to direct it in the ways of spiritual progress. His success depends primarily on his knowledge of spiritual matters, his ability

[1] Canon 888, § 1.

[2] Voltas, "De aperienda, directionis causa, Superioribus conscientia"—*CpR,* I (1920), 83; Merkelbach, *Summa Theologiae Moralis* (3 vols., Vol. III, 2. ed., 1936), III, nn. 608–613.

to impart this knowledge and the influence of his personality and example on others. The personal qualities of the spiritual director are very important, inasmuch as his influence on others is more personal than ministerial. His effectiveness proceeds *ex opere operantis*, that is, in accordance with the value of the agent's work and action.

Article I. The Confessions of Religious in the Pre-Code Law

The IV General Council of the Lateran (1215) prescribed that parishioners were to make their paschal confession to their own proper pastor or his delegate.[3] The proper pastor for the religious of a clerical institute was considered to be the Superior of the monastery or his delegate.[4]

In 1593 Clement VIII forbade religious Superiors to hear the confessions of their subjects unless the penitents had committed some reserved sin, or unless they spontaneously approached the Superior for making their confession. At the same time Superiors were commanded to appoint two or three or even more confessors in each monastery to hear the confessions of the religious subject to them. Those designated could absolve from reserved cases if they considered it imprudent to approach the Superior for the necessary faculty.[5] Ten years later the same Pope made the Master of novices the ordinary confessor of the novices. The local Superior, however, could hear the confessions of the novices once or twice in the year.[6]

From the time of these two papal documents the Superior of the monastery was not allowed to act as the ordinary confessor of the religious or the novices. If the Superior at the same time fulfilled the office of the Master of novices, he was the ordinary confessor of the novices.

---

[3] C. 12, X, *de poenitentiis et remissionibus*, V. 38.

[4] Suarez, *Omnia opera* (ed. nova, 28 vols., Parisiis, *De religione*, tr. VIII, lib. II, cap. XV, n. 3; Vermeersch, "De unitate confessarii ordinarii apud Moniales et Sorores"—*Periodica de Re Canonica et Morali utili praesertim Religiosis et Missionariis* (Brugis, 1905–) V (1913), (1)–(12).

[5] Const., "*Sanctissimus*," 26 maii 1593, §§ 2, 3—*Fontes*, n. 177.

[6] Const., "*Cum ad regularem*," 19 mart. 1603, § 10—*Fontes*, n. 189.

The Sacred Congregation of Bishops and Regulars in 1866 decreed that in every religious community, no matter how small, at least one confessor should be designated to hear the confessions of the religious.[7] Many clerical non-exempt congregations had arisen after the Council of Trent. Being under the Bishop as regards jurisdiction, these religious could go to confession to any priest who possessed diocesan faculties. It was disputed whether regulars also could validly confess to a confessor not approved by the religious Superior.[8]

The Holy Office on July 5, 1899, prohibited Superiors of religious communities, seminaries and colleges in the city of Rome from hearing the confessions of subjects except in case of necessity.[9] This was a step beyond the Clementine legislation. According to the latter, the religious subject could confess to the Superior if the action was spontaneous on the part of the subject. In August, 1899, the Holy Office responded that the decree of the preceding July did not affect the Apostolic Constitutions of Clement VIII, and that the law for confessors in the monastery of regulars remained unchanged,[10] inasmuch as this decree of the Holy Office was meant for religious congregations of simple vows.

In the Constitution *Cum ad regularem* Clement VIII ruled that the Master of novices was to be the ordinary confessor of the novices. This Pontiff also had issued an earlier decree in which he provided for the appointment of confessors for the professed religious, and ordered that not the Superiors, but the priests designated by the Superiors were to act in the capacity of the regular confessor for the community. The Superior could hear the confession of a subject who of his own accord made the request. Following the year 1899, in congregations of simple vows, a Superior, even when requested by his subjects, could hear their confessions only in case of some real necessity. This was certainly

[7] S. C. super Statu Regularium, 17 aug. 1866—*Fontes,* n. 4389.

[8] Shuhler, *Privileges of Regulars to Absolve and Dispense,* The Catholic University of America Canon Law Studies, n. 186 (Washington, D. C.: The Catholic University of America Press, 1943), pp. 50–56.

[9] S. C. S. Off., 5 iul. 1899—*Fontes,* n. 1225.

[10] S. C. S. Off., 23 aug. 1899—*Acta Sanctae Sedis* (41 vols., Romae, 1865–1908), XXXII (1899), 253.

the law for the city of Rome, and very probably also the practice which was followed by most of the congregations of simple vows throughout the world. Thus the sphere in which the local Superior and the Master of novices were allowed to act in the matter of their subject's confessions was clearly defined. But to which one of these officials was the Superior of the students compared? Was he bound by the legislation which governed the rights of the local Superior, or by that which regulated the province of the Master of novices?

The answer to this question depends on the solution of another problem, namely, the status of the Superior of the students in the community. The conclusion already reached in this study is that he was a Superior only in the wide sense of the term, and was likened to the Master of novices inasmuch as he carried on the work begun in the novitiate by the Master of novices. His authority was greatly restricted when compared with that of the local Superior. Since he was not the local Superior, it seems that he was not included in the legislation of Clement VIII, which forbade the Superior to hear the confessions of the religious subjects. Furthermore, the duty of the Superior of the students was to continue the work of the Master of novices, and because of the analogy between his office and that of the Master of novices he was able to act as ordinary confessor for the students, for such a procedure was in harmony with the legislation of the time which made the Master of novices the ordinary confessor of the novices.

Finally, it should be recalled that the junior religious could also follow the legislation of Clement VIII which was given for the benefit of the entire community. This legislation permitted the religious to choose an ordinary confessor from one of those appointed for the community, unless the Constitutions of a particular order ruled otherwise.[11]

Article II. The Spiritual Prefect as Ordinary Confessor of the Students

A. The Spiritual Prefect with Power According to Canon 588

Concerning the province of the Spiritual Prefect as confessor

[11] Piat, *Praelectiones Iuris Regularium,* I, 112.

for the clerical religious students the Code is silent. There is no reference to his office in the Code except in canon 588, §§ 1, 2, where his qualities and duties are enumerated. In this canon the law does not specify whether the Spiritual Prefect is permitted to act as the ordinary confessor of the students.

It is, however, the opinion of canonical writers that the Spiritual Prefect may be appointed as the confessor of the students, unless this is forbidden by particular law, or unless authority in the external forum over the students is entrusted to him. But according to the common law itself, they say, there is no prohibition placed on the Spiritual Prefect to forbid him to hear the confessions of the students. The reasons given to prove that the office of confessor may be assumed by the Spiritual Prefect are: (a) the appointment is not forbidden by the *law* of the Code; (b) the appointment is not contrary to the *mind* of the legislator; (c) the office of confessor is compatible with the duties of the Spiritual Prefect; and (d) the opinion is approved by the authority of the canonists.

(a) Religious Superiors are indeed forbidden in the Code to hear the confessions of their religious subjects, unless the latter by their own spontaneous choice request it. Further, the Code also requires that if the religious choose to confess habitually to their Superiors, a grave cause must be present.[12] In like manner the Code forbids the Master of novices, his Assistant, and the Superior of a seminary or a college to receive the sacramental confessions of the youths living in the same house with them, unless the youths, moved by a grave and urgent cause, spontaneously request in particular cases to make their confession to any of these officials.[13]

The Spiritual Prefect does not fall under the prohibition enacted by the law either in canon 518, § 2, or in canon 891. He does not fall under the law enacted in canon 518, § 2, since he is not a superior in the strict sense as contemplated by that canon. In it the term *Superior* is used in the strict sense. It includes only those who are Superiors in the sense of the Code, namely major and minor Superiors. The term is not extended to others, not

[12] Canon 518, § 2.

[13] Canon 891.

even to those who may possess some authority in the external rule of the community, but is limited to the major and minor Superiors. By no means does the term Superior in canon 518, § 2, include the Spiritual Prefect.[14] Neither is the Spiritual Prefect to be identified with those who are mentioned in canon 891, namely, the Master of novices, his Assistant, or the Superior of a seminary or a college, although he may perform duties in some respects similar to the duties of the Master of novices and the Assistant Master. He is therefore not forbidden by the Code to hear the confessions of the religious clerical students either in particular cases or even habitually.

(b) Further, it is not contrary to the mind of the legislator that the Spiritual Prefect should be appointed as ordinary confessor. Throughout the Code there is a distinct separation of the external and internal forums in religious communities, which is upheld not only in theory but in practice.[15]

The Master of novices has authority in the external forum, and therefore it was to be expected that according to the present policy of the legislator he would be explicitly excluded from exercising ordinary authority in the internal sacramental forum.[16] Likewise the major and minor Superiors have the government in the external forum entrusted to them. The legislator, in preserving the separation of the forums, allows the religious to confess to their superiors only under certain conditions. The Spiritual Prefect is not entrusted with the external government of the clerical students, but with their spiritual formation and their spiritual supervision. His authority by reason of the common law is limited to the internal forum.[17] As a consequence, Superiors would not be acting contrary to the *mind* of the legislator if they appointed the Spiritual Prefect among the ordinary confessors of the religious students, for the Spiritual Prefect does not exercise authority in the external forum according to the common law.

(c) It is the duty of the Spiritual Prefect to form the souls of the clerical religious students by instructions, exhortations and

---

[14] Larraona "Consultationes"—*CpR,* I (1920), 54, 55.

[15] Cf. canons 518, § 2, 530; 891.

[16] Canon 891.

[17] *Supra*, pp. 33–38.

admonitions, to encourage and develop solid virtue in the spiritual life of the student. General instructions and general direction to the clerics as a group are indeed useful in promoting the sanctity and virtue of the individual clerics. But, if this is so, it is obvious that personal instruction and personal direction imparted to each individual religious are marked by even greater utility and importance in their progress in the spiritual life. This individual direction is compatible with and is supplemented by its union with the internal sacramental forum. The internal forum, sacramental and extra-sacramental, work harmoniously together and make for the spiritual benefit of the student.

(d) The common opinion of the authors is that the Spiritual Prefect is not forbidden by the common law to act as the confessor of the students.[18] Goyeneche is opposed to this opinion.[19] While admitting that canons 518, § 2, and 891 according to their liberal meaning do not forbid the Spiritual Prefect to hear the confessions of the students, nevertheless he contends that the practice of hearing the students' confessions is contrary to the mind of the legislator. His opposition to the practice of the Spiritual Prefect's hearing the confessions of the students arises from this acknowledged parity between the office of the Master of novices and that of the Spiritual Prefect. He maintains that the Spiritual Prefect is ruled by the same norms as the Master of novices. This parity he traces back to the time of Clement VIII, as can be seen, so he asserts, in the Constitutions of the Order of Preachers.[20]

The argument of Goyeneche is based on his contention that there is a parity between the offices of the Master of novices and the Spiritual Prefect, and that the Spiritual Prefect is to be considered as one having authority in the external forum. If they

[18] Berutti, *Institutiones,* III, n. 100; Coronata, *Institutiones,* I, n. 597; Toso, *Commentaria Minora,* V, 163; Fanfani, *De Iure Religiosorum,* n. 276; Prümmer, *Manuale,* p. 288; Larraona, "Consultationes"—*CpR,* I (1920), 52, (6); Beste, *Introductio in Codicem,* p. 400; Canuto, "De regimine domus studiorum in religione clericali exempta ad normam can. 588"—*Apollinaris* IX (1936), 33, 34.

[19] "Consultationes"—*CpR,* VII (1926), 183, 184.

[20] *Constitutiones Fratrum S. Ordinis Praedicatorum* (ed. nova, Parisiis, 1886), nn. 1052, 1054.

both have authority in the external forum, and the Spiritual Prefect rules the students in the same way or almost in the same way as the Master rules the novices, then there is to be admitted the parity for which Goyeneche contends, and according to the policy of the present law the Spiritual Prefect would be forbidden to hear the confessions of the students.[21] If the Spiritual Prefect does not have authority in the external forum, the asserted parity does not exist. According to the opinion defended in this work, the Spiritual Prefect does not have any power in the external government of the community except such as is granted to him by particular law. Consequently, he is not forbidden by the canons of the Code in consequence of the mind of the legislator to hear, even by way of ordinary practice, the sacramental confessions of the clerical professed students.

B. THE SPIRITUAL PREFECT WITH AUTHORITY IN THE EXTERNAL FORUM UNDER PARTICULAR LAW

It is possible that in some religious institutes the Spiritual Prefect will have bestowed upon him some authority in the external forum while at the same time he will continue to exercise his duties in the internal forum. The authority in the internal forum proceeds from the common law, the power in the external forum arises from particular law. When authority in both forums is vested in the Spiritual Prefect, may he exercise the office of ordinary confessor for the students?

Several distinctions must be made at this point. While it is true that there exists in the common law today a policy in regard to the confessions of novices [22] different from that of the days of Clement VIII,[23] when the Master of novices was the recognized ordinary confessor of the novices, nevertheless even under the present law the novice may approach the Master of novices in the sacrament of Penance in particular cases when a grave and urgent cause is present.[24] In like manner there is a notable difference between the present law and that of the time of the IV

[21] Canon 891.

[22] Canons 556, § 2; 891.

[23] Const., "*Cum ad regularem,*" 19 mart. 1603, § 10—*Fontes,* n. 189.

[24] Canon 891.

General Lateran Council, according to the prescriptions of which the proper pastor to receive the confessions of the religious was considered to be the Superior of the monastery or his delegate.[25] But even today the religious may confess habitually to the Superior for a grave cause, and they may confess occasionally for no other reason than their own preference, provided that they act freely and are not physically or morally constrained by the Superior.[26] Hence, while the separation of the sacramental forum and the external forum is more strictly maintained than at the time of the IV General Lateran Council, or even at the time of Clement VIII, still the separation is not so absolute as *always* to forbid the subject to approach the Superior as his confessor.

The opinion of most of the canonists who specifically treat the subject is that the Spiritual Prefect with authority by delegation in the external forum may not act as the ordinary confessor of the students. The reason for this opinion is based on the policy of the present law in preserving the separation between the sacramental forum and that of the external government. This opinion is explicitly stated by several authors.[27] The principle of separation is followed by the legislator and expressly stated in canons 518 and 530. But since the legislator does not expressly state whether or not the Spiritual Prefect may hear the confessions of the students when he exercises authority over them in the external forum, it is necessary, therefore, to seek a guiding norm for this situation from laws enacted in similar cases.[28]

If, then, it is forbidden for the Spiritual Prefect with authority over the external discipline to hear the confession of the students, one may further determine whether the prohibition is to be specifically sought in canon 518, §§ 2, 3, which concerns the Superiors, or in canon 891, which pertains to the Master of novices. For, if the prohibition arises according to canon 518, §§ 2, 3, the stu-

---

[25] Suarez, *De religione,* tr. VIII, lib. II, cap. XV, n. 3.

[26] Canon 519, §§ 2, 3.

[27] Vermeersch-Creusen, *Epitome,* I, n. 741; Coronata, *Institutiones,* I, n. 597; Larraona, "Consultationes"—*CpR,* I (1920), 53, (6); Goyeneche, "Consultationes" —*CpR,* VII (1926), 183, 184; Langasco, "De regimine domus studiorum in religione clericali"—*JP,* XIX (1939), 55–69.

[28] Canon 20.

dents may confess to the Spiritual Prefect habitually as long as a grave cause exists, and occasionally without such a grave cause provided that they act spontaneously in the matter. But, if the prohibition derives from canon 891, then a grave and urgent cause must be present for the student to confess to the Spiritual Prefect even in a particular case.

The Spiritual Prefect, when he has an assignment to govern the house of studies in disciplinary matters as well as to supervise the spiritual formation of the students, will be responsible for the external conduct and the formation of character in the students in almost the same manner as the Master of novices is held responsible for his duties. When the Spiritual Prefect must also give a report to the Superiors and the Chapter on the conduct of the students, and when his testimony is considered to be the most important of all and is employed as a guide to be followed by the Superiors and the Chapter, then he acts in the same manner as the Master of novices. In such a case a parity does indeed exist between the two offices. Consequently, where the same reason prevails, there, too, the same prescription of law should prevail.[29] When this parity exists between the offices of the Master of novices and the Spiritual Prefect, it seems that canon 891 is the law that is applicable to the latter, and the students may not confess to the Spiritual Prefect except in a particular case for a grave and urgent cause, such as the tranquility of conscience (here is the grave cause) which is to be achieved shortly before the reception of Holy Communion (here is the urgent cause).

Larraona,[30] on the contrary, thinks that the Spiritual Prefect who has authority over the discipline of the house of studies should be considered more after the manner of a Superior than likened to the Master of novices. However, much depends on the degree of authority vested in the Spiritual Prefect. If the latter exercises his authority with great dependence on the local Superior, he seems to come under the enactments of canon 518, §§ 2, 3, inasmuch as he does not possess that independence which

---

[29] Goyeneche, "Consultationes"—*CpR,* VII (1926), 183, 184.

[30] "Consultationes"—*CpR,* I (1920), 52, (6).

is proper to the Master of novices.[31] In each case it is necessary, first, to decide whether the Spiritual Prefect proceeds after the manner of the local Superior or after the manner of the Master of novices. Having arrived at a satisfactory conclusion, one may then apply the respective canons 518, §§ 2, 3 and 891.

Finally, there is the opinion of Schaefer[32] which denies that relative to the prohibition of hearing the students' confession, there is an obligation arising either from canon 518, §§ 2, 3, or from canon 891. He recognizes the parity existing between the offices of the Master of novices and the Spiritual Prefect when both have authority in the external forum, and he admits that it is the mind of the legislator that he who has charge of the external government should not retain control in the sacramental forum. But he says that the legislator has made no express determination concerning the Spiritual Prefect, and therefore the liberty of the latter should not be curtailed as long as a prohibition does not clearly exist.

It is true that the legislator has not included in the Code any canon which decides the case under consideration by expressly mentioning the name of the Spiritual Prefect. Nevertheless, he has furnished general principles in the light of which one may determine a norm of action in the cases not specifically provided for by the law.[33] Consequently, when the Spiritual Prefect possesses authority over the external government of the house of studies, he bears a marked resemblance to the Superior and the Master of novices inasmuch as all alike are endowed with external authority, although one may differ from the other in the degree of the authority to be exercised by him. Since the Spiritual Prefect in the case under consideration possesses authority in the external forum, and since the policy of the separation of the sacramental and external forum is a principle of the present law, it follows that the reason which forbids the Superior and the Master of novices to hear the confessions of their subjects also prevails in the case of the Spiritual Prefect, and consequently the latter is bound by the same norms in his procedure.

[31] Canon 561, § 1.

[32] *De Religiosis*, p. 635.

[33] Canon 20.

C. CUSTOM

What may be said of the custom by which the Spiritual Prefect is the ordinary confessor of the students? In the first place, it is necessary in each institute which has such a custom to consult the Constitutions which have been approved since the promulgation of the Code to discover whether the custom has received approbation. Secondly, if the question is not settled by the Constitutions, several matters must be taken into account before a decision can be rendered.

According to the Constitution *Cum ad regularem,*[34] a priest whose work it was to train the students was assigned in the same manner in which there was appointed a Master of novices whose task it was to have charge of the novices. Now, the Master of novices was appointed as the ordinary confessor of the novices. In like manner, then, the priest who had charge of the students became the ordinary confessor for the students.

In the present law the Master of novices is not permitted to be the ordinary confessor of the novices, and the latter may approach the Master only when a grave and urgent cause is present in a particular case.[35] When the Spiritual Prefect possesses authority in the external forum and exercises his office in almost the same manner as the Master, he is forbidden by canon 891 to hear the confessions of the novices because of the similarity between his office and that of the Master, just as he was allowed to hear the confession of the students before the present law, and for the same reason. The prohibition comes by reason of canon 20 [36] inasmuch as the norm for the Spiritual Prefect arises through an application of the suppletive rule of interpretation enunciated in this canon. Consequently the custom of his hearing the confessions of the students is not only against the mind of the legislator, but also against the law of the Code, and must be judged

[34] Clemens VIII, 19 mart. 1603, § 20—*Fontes,* n. 189.

[35] Canon 891.

[36] " Si certa de re desit expressum praescriptum legis sive generalis sive particularis, norma sumenda est, nisi agatur de poenis applicandis a legibus latis in similibus; a generalibus iuris principiis cum aequitate canonica servatis; a stylo et praxi Curiae Romanae; a communi constantique sententia doctorum."

according to the principles of canon 5 if it antedated the Code, and according to canons 25–30 if it is subsequent to the Code.

If the custom of the Spiritual Prefect receiving the confessions of the students when he possessed external authority flourished for less than a hundred years before the Code, it was abrogated when the Code became binding law in 1918.[37] If the custom had more than a hundred years' existence at the advent of the Code, it remained for the Ordinary to tolerate the continuance of that custom if he judged that it could not prudently be suppressed. There seems little reason for tolerating such a custom, since no objection would arise on the part of the students, for they are the ones who would chiefly benefit on account of the greater liberty of conscience allowed to them. If the custom arose since the promulgation of the Code, sufficient time has not elapsed to give legal sanction to the practice of the Spiritual Prefect's hearing the confessions of the students in those institutes in which he governs the external discipline of the house of studies.[38]

Article III. The Appointment of the Spiritual Prefect as Confessor

Since the Spiritual Prefect is not forbidden by common law or by the practice of the Church to hear the confessions of the students as long as he possesses no authority in the external forum, the Superior may designate him as one of the ordinary confessors of the community.[39] In an exempt religious community the designation and the granting of jurisdiction are acts reserved to the religious Superiors according to the Constitutiones.[40] In a non-exempt religious clerical community the designation is reserved to the religious Superior, but the concession of jurisdiction pertains to the local Ordinary.[41]

If the Spiritual Prefect is forbidden to receive the confessions of the students when he has authority over them in disciplinary

[37] Canon 5.

[38] Canon 27, § 1.

[39] Canons 518, § 1; 875, § 1.

[40] Canon 875, § 1.

[41] Canons 518, § 1; 874, § 1.

matters, he may, nevertheless, be appointed as one of the ordinary confessors of the religious community, provided that at least two other confessors are placed at the disposal of the students. The reason for this statement is based on the legislation contained in canon 518, § 1, which demands that more than a single confessor (*plures confessarii*) be appointed in every clerical house. The students as well as the older religious have the right to choose from at least two. This right would be denied the students if the Spiritual Prefect were one of the two confessors. Larraona [42] interprets "*plures*" to have reference to at least two.

If the Master of novices fulfills the duties of the Spiritual Prefect with authority over the students in the external discipline, he may not hear the confessions of the students, although he may act as confessor for the other members of the community.

Article IV. The Manifestation of Conscience

A. Definition

Manifestation of conscience may be described as the disclosure of one's state of mind and soul by revealing one's virtues, defects, temptations, trials, passions, difficulties, doubts, inclinations, intentions, in order that the person to whom the disclosure is made may acquire a satisfactory knowledge of one's spiritual condition and lead the way to one's spiritual perfection.[43]

The revelation is called precisely a manifestation of conscience, for it reveals to another those acts and inclinations which no one else has witnessed. It is a disclosure of likes and dislikes for certain occupations, of the progress made in prayer, of antipathies towards persons. Not every disclosure of one's state of mind to another is a manifestation of conscience in the sense here understood. Here it signifies the revelation of the state of one's unwitnessed spiritual, mental and moral processes under secrecy for the purpose of obtaining spiritual direction and help. To manifest publicly or privately, according to the Constitutions, the external violation of a rule—a practice followed in many religious com-

[42] "Commentarium Codicis"—*CpR*, X (1929), 252.

[43] Vermeersch-Creusen, *Epitome*, I, n. 650; Larraona, "Commentarium Codicis"—*CpR*, XII (1931), 128; Berutti, *Institutiones*, III, n. 55.

munities—is not a manifestation of conscience in the strict sense here outlined. A confession of the external faults is a manifestation only of the external act of violating a rule, not a disclosure of the state of soul that accompanied the external act.[44]

The purpose of making the manifestation of conscience is to obtain help and direction from men experienced in leading souls to perfection. The good that is directly and immediately sought is the spiritual good of the individual, although the good of the institute may also be promoted indirectly and secondarily by way of improvement in the cõnduct of the religious.[45]

Manifestation of conscience is considered to be an act of the internal extra-sacramental forum. Nevertheless the act of manifestation of conscience may be combined with the act of confession. If this happens, then the priest in receiving both revelations assumes the twofold rôle of confessor and director.[46] The law in regard to the manifestation of conscience in its precise and strict meaning will be considered, first, as it existed before the Code and, secondly, as it exists today.

B. THE DECREE "QUEMADMODUM"

In 1890 the Sacred Congregation of Bishops and Regulars deplored the evils that had arisen in some institutes of women religious and of lay institutes of men religious concerning the manifestation of conscience because of the abuse of it on the part of Superiors. The decree stated that originally the manifestation of conscience was permitted in some institutes in order that the members might the more easily progress towards perfection by disclosing their difficulties to the Superiors and receiving a solution of them, but instead the subjects had actually been hindered in their spiritual progress because the Superiors forced from them the revelation of matters that were strictly reserved to the sacrament of Penance. As a consequence there resulted anxiety of soul on the part of the religious, and disturbance of the peace of the community through rifts and discord.[47]

---

[44] Vermeersch-Creusen, *Epitome,* I, n. 650.

[45] Larraona, "Commentarium Codicis"—*CpR,* XII (1931), 128.

[46] Voltas, "De aperienda, directionis causa, Superioribus conscientia"—*CpR,* I (1920), 84.

[47] S. C. Ep. et Reg., decr. *"Quemadmodum,"* 17 dec. 1890—*Fontes,* n. 2017.

The decree *Quemadmodum* revoked all the prescriptions of the Constitutions of women religious and lay institutes of men religious which required a manifestation of conscience, even though the Constitutions had been approved *in forma specialissima*. Any customs, even immemorial, to the contrary were also abrogated.[48]

Furthermore, all Superiors of the above named institutes were strictly forbidden by the decree to induce in any manner a manifestation of conscience from the persons subject to them. The phrase " in any manner " was explained in detail to mean directly or indirectly, by precept, counsel, fear, threats or flattery. In case of a violation of the decree, subjects were commanded to denounce minor Superiors to the major Superiors, the major Superiors to the Sacred Congregation of Bishops and Regulars.[49]

Finally, under the decree, subjects were allowed to open their minds to their Superiors for the purpose of obtaining counsel and direction in doubts and anxieties. But they were to possess the greatest freedom in this matter and could not be constrained by any Superior.[50]

In this decree there is no reference to *clerical* religious. The decree *Quemadmodum* did not apply to them, but only to institutes of women religious and lay institutes of men religious. Not until the promulgation of the Code were the prescriptions of the decree *Quemadmodum* applied also to institutes of clerical religious. The present law together with its variations from the decree *Quemadmodum* appropriately presents itself for immediate consideration.

C. THE CODE OF CANON LAW

Canon 530, §§ 1, 2, treats of the manifestation of conscience. The Code law is at once an extension and a restriction of the earlier law. It is an extension, because the prohibition which is stated in canon 530, § 1, is directed not to women religious and lay men religious only, but to *all* religious institutes including clerical religious. The Code at the same time restricts the decree

---

[48] S. C. Ep. et Reg., decr. "*Quemadmodum*," § 1—*Fontes*, n. 2017.
[49] S. C. Ep. et Reg., decr. "*Quemadmodum*," § 2—*Fontes*, n. 2017.
[50] S. C. Ep. et Reg., decr. "*Quemadmodum*," § 3—*Fontes*, n. 2017.

Quemadmodum, because the present law does not require subjects to report violations of the law.

Canon 530, § 1. Omnes religiosi Superiores districte vetantur personas sibi subditas quoquo modo inducere ad conscientiae manifestationem sibi peragendam.

The phrase "*omnes religiosi Superiores*" embraces all those who according to the law are considered Superiors, general, provincial and local, men and women. According to many authors [51] the term "Superior" is to be taken in the strict sense, and is not to be extended to those who in a wide sense are called Superiors, as, for instance, the Assistant to the local Superior. Berutti [52] asserts that the phrase "*omnes religiosi Superiores*" embraces every Superior who from common or particular law has dominative power by reason of his office. Thus he says that the Master of novices and, under certain circumstances, the Spiritual Prefect are included under the law of canon 530, § 1, according to the wording of the law; the Master of novices, because from common law he is entrusted with the government of the novices, and the Spiritual Prefect, when according to the Constitutions he is entrusted with the rule of the students in almost the same way as the Master is entrusted with the rule of the novices. His reason is based on the terminology of canon 530, § 1, which employs the words "omnes religiosi Superiores . . . personas sibi subditas." He points out that this terminology is very broad and includes all kinds of Superiors. Furthermore, he says, it mentions *persons subject* to the Superiors, and not simply religious subject to Superiors.

The opinion, then, followed by most of the canonists maintains that the Spiritual Prefect by reason of the common law does not fall under the prohibition enacted in canon 530, § 1. Even Berutti does not disagree if the sole consideration is the office of the

---

[51] Larraona, "Commentarium Codicis"—*CpR,* XII (1931), 126; Vermeersch-Creusen, *Epitome,* I, n. 650; Voltas, "De aperienda, directionis causa, Superioribus conscientia"—*CpR,* I (1920), 148; Goyeneche, "Consultationes"—*CpR,* V (1924), 160; Schaefer, *De Religiosis,* p. 635; Wernz-Vidal, *Ius Canonicum,* III, n. 213; Ferreres, *Institutiones,* I, n. 840; Beste, *Introductio in Codicem,* p. 349; Coronata, *Institutiones,* I, n. 557.

[52] *Institutiones,* III, n. 55.

Spiritual Prefect as exclusively contemplated in the common law.

If the Spiritual Prefect has authority in the external forum, he may seek a manifestation of conscience from the students, Goyeneche says, provided that he uses persuasion and suggestion, and not force and fear. The reason for this view is based on the peculiar duty of the Master of novices and the Spiritual Prefect, both of whom exercise an office different from that of the local Superior. Their duty is to form character in the souls of their charges by means of their study of the Rules and Constitutions, by means also of pious meditation, of assiduous prayer, and of attention to those matters which pertain to the vows and virtues.[53]

The aim of both the Spiritual Prefect and the Master of novices can be realized better when a manifestation of conscience is made to them by their respective subjects. Vermeersch-Creusen[54] assert that such a manifestation on the part of the novices is necessary for the proper training of the novices. It seems that the same reason can be applied here if the Spiritual Prefect has charge of the students in a similar manner. However, it must always be remembered that the Code places no obligation on novices or students to reveal their innermost spiritual life.

By way of conclusion it may be said in this regard that even the Spiritual Prefect who has authority in the external forum by particular law is permitted to urge in the manner of a kindly request or of a gracious invitation a manifestation of conscience from the students. Through his receiving of this manifestation he becomes better able to aid the student who may be weighed down with doubts, difficulties and temptations, which may endanger his vocation and impede the very spiritual progress which it is the duty of the Spiritual Prefect to promote. The students, however, have no obligation to accede to the request, and the Spiritual Prefect may not change his attitude toward those who seek assistance from others.

---

[53] Canon 565, § 1. This canon pertains to the Master of novices. It can be applied by analogy to the Spiritual Prefect when he governs the students in the same manner as the Master rules the novices.

[54] *Epitome,* I, n. 650.

CHAPTER VIII

THE SPIRITUAL PREFECT AND THE USE OF KNOWLEDGE

ARTICLE I. SOURCES OF KNOWLEDGE

If the Spiritual Prefect receives the sacramental confessions of some or all of the students, he will obtain an intimate knowledge of the spiritual condition of their souls. Likewise, if he is given a manifestation of conscience by some or all of the students, he will know if they are worthy or unworthy to proceed to the profession of perpetual vows and the reception of minor and major orders. Furthermore, the Spiritual Prefect, because of his residence in the same monastery with the students and his frequent association with them, will acquire definite impressions of the students from an observation of them in the discharge of their duties. Thus he may possess knowledge of the students from three sources, namely, (a) from the sacrament of Penance, (b) from the manifestation of conscience, (c) from observation. How is the Spiritual Director to act in regard to the use of knowledge from one or two or all three of these sources?

ARTICLE II. THE USE OF CONFESSIONAL KNOWLEDGE

A. DIRECT AND INDIRECT VIOLATION OF THE SEAL

Canon 889, § 1, in stating that the sacramental seal is always inviolable, forbids the confessor in any manner or for any cause to betray the penitent by a revelation of his sins. This canon prohibits by ecclesiastical law what already is forbidden by divine natural and divine positive law.[1] Under the sacramental seal falls that knowledge which, if revealed, would manifest the sinner as

[1] Merkelbach, *Summa Theologiae Moralis,* III, n. 621; Aertnys-Damen, *Theologia Moralis secundum Doctrinam S. Alfonsi De Ligorio Doct. Ecclesiae* (2 vols., 13. ed., Taurini—Romae: Marietti, 1939), II, n. 455. Hereafter cited as *Theologia Moralis.*

such, or create the proximate danger of manifesting him as such, or render the sacrament of Penance odious.[2]

The confessor may never violate the seal of confession. The obligation of secrecy urges in every conceivable instance unless or until the penitent has given his free and certain consent which allows the confessor to disclose the matter of confession.[3] The obligation to respect the seal urges even though through its violation the greatest benefits would result for the penitent himself, for the confessor, for a third party, or for the State, the Church, or religion in general. Consequently, the Spiritual Prefect, when acting in the rôle of confessor for the clerical students, cannot make use of his confessional knowledge to reveal an unworthy candidate in order to prevent the Church from suffering a great injury, even though it were the plague of heresy.[4] The Spiritual Prefect in dealing with a penitent in the confessional grants or denies absolution according to the good disposition or bad disposition of the penitent. He must maintain silence, even though the cleric advances unworthily to the perpetual profession of vows and the reception of minor and major orders.

B. THE USE OF KNOWLEDGE WITHOUT VIOLATION OF THE SEAL

The Spiritual Prefect as a confessor may never directly or indirectly violate the seal of confession. But may he use knowledge obtained from confession when there is no danger of the violation of the seal and no likelihood of any emergence of scandal?

In such a case it is permitted to use knowledge from confession, provided that the penitent suffers no harm, and provided, further, that neither the individual penitent nor penitents in general derive from such a use of knowledge a sense of personal grievance, a consciousness of betrayed trust, or even the persuasion of an impending injury which may be sustained by themselves or by others.[5] Cappello[6] says that the words " cum gravamine poeni-

---

[2] Merkelbach, *Summa Theologiae Moralis*, III, n. 625.

[3] Merkelbach, *Summa Theologiae Moralis*, III, n. 622; Aertnys-Damen, *Theologia Moralis*, II, n. 455.

[4] Merkelbach, *Summa Theologiae Moralis*, III, n. 622.

[5] Merkelbach, *Summa Theologiae Moralis*, III, n. 628; Aertnys-Damen, *Theologia Moralis*, II, n. 462; Cappello, *Tractatus Canonico-Moralis de*

tentis" in canon 890, § 1, must be understood as referring to all penitents, and not only to the one who has actually made his confession. Thus, in order that the confessor may rightly use the knowledge obtained by him in confession, he must be certain of the verification of the following conditions: that neither a direct nor an indirect violation of the seal is involved, that there is no probability for the arising of scandal, that no harm is occasioned for the particular penitent, that neither the individual penitent nor penitents in general will with any likelihood suffer any sense of personal grievance, of betrayed trust, or of impending injury, vexation or annoyance for themselves or for others. It is the confessor's right, which in its exercise postulates a profound sense of responsibility, to judge whether all these conditions are verified.

The Spiritual Prefect acting as a confessor for the students would cause annoyance to them if he spoke to them outside the confessional of matters learned in the confessional, if in the conferences he mentioned particular sins of particular penitents, even apart of course from the emergence of any danger of the violation of the seal, or if he adopted an attitude of coldness toward the penitent after hearing the latter's confession.[7] On the other hand, the Spiritual Prefect may use the knowledge obtained in confession to advance his own progress in the spiritual life, to pray for his penitents, to study more zealously in the future in order to become more competent.[8]

When the Spiritual Prefect is entrusted with the *external* government of the students, he may not use knowledge obtained from the confession of the students for regulating the life of the community.[9] This is an application of the second paragraph of canon 890 which forbids the use of confessional knowledge "cum gravamine poenitentis." This canon, it must be remembered, does

---

Sacramentis (Vol. II, pars 1, 2, ed., Romae: Marietti, 1928), n. 914. Hereafter cited as *De Sacramentis.*

[6] *De Sacramentis,* II[1], n. 914.

[7] Cf. Merkelbach, *Summa Theologiae Moralis,* III, n. 628. Aertnys-Damen, *Moralis Theologia,* II, 464.

[8] Merkelbach, *Summa Theologiae Moralis,* III, n. 628.

[9] Canon 890, § 2.

not specifically speak of *religious* superiors, but simply treats of superiors who are placed in charge of the external government. Consequently, if the Spiritual Prefect has authority in the external forum vested in him, he is forbidden by reason of canon 890, § 2, to use confessional knowledge in the external government of the students. The prohibition derives also from the very nature of his office, for the reason that the penitents would feel aggrieved if they knew that the matter of confession could be used in the external government of the community.[10] After hearing the confession of a student, therefore, the Spiritual Prefect may not, in consequence of the confession, change the assignments of the students, show preference to one rather than to others, or indicate by his actions that he has heard the confession of a student.

Article III. The Use of Knowledge Received from a Manifestation of Conscience

A. Definition of Terms

The knowledge obtained by a Superior or by the Spiritual Prefect from the manifestation of conscience by the religious is a natural and committed secret. This knowledge contains elements resulting from a disclosure of the inmost life of a person, the thoughts and inclinations which are entirely hidden from others. The manifestation of these thoughts and inclinations is given to another with the implicit understanding that secrecy will be observed. This knowledge is considered by him to be secret.

There is no law in the Code concerning the use of knowledge acquired outside the confessional. Hence it is necessary to resort to general moral principles and to the instructions of the Holy See in order to discover the extent to which the possessor of secret knowledge is bound to its observance.

A secret, subjectively considered, is the *obligation* of not manifesting some hidden matter, while objectively considered it is the hidden matter itself. A secret may be natural, promised or committed according as the obligation to respect it arises from different sources. A *natural* secret is one whose obligation arises

[10] Cf. Cappello, *De Sacramentis*, II[1], n. 928.

from the very nature of the matter, which is such that it cannot be disclosed without causing some injury to another. A *promised* secret is one whose obligation arises by reason of one's word of honor to safeguard knowledge already possessed. A *committed* secret is one whose obligation arises from a pact by which the person receives information unknown before, under the expressed or tacit condition of keeping the information from others. This agreement may be expressed in words, or based on a fact from which it is obvious that knowledge is given in secret, as in the case of knowledge imparted to professional men.[11]

Not all committed secrets impose the same obligation to maintain secrecy. A committed secret between private citizens does not impose the same obligation as a secret entrusted to a public official.[12] The latter kind of secret must be kept by reason of the public good. Knowledge received from a manifestation of conscience is of this kind, and correspondingly imposes a very strict obligation on the recipient. The secret knowledge thus committed to him is sometimes called quasi-sacramental.[13]

To reveal licitly a committed secret it is required that the revelation of it be necessary as a means for avoiding a proportionately grave loss.[14] To manifest a secret entrusted by reason of office requires a graver cause than to reveal a secret entrusted to an individual whose status does not involve any official capacity, the reason being that the common good always suffers to at least some degree in the former case. Finally, an obligation arising by reason of the common good to observe secrecy ceases when the same common good demands a disclosure of the knowledge.[15] These principles must be kept in mind if one is properly to determine the obligations of the Superior and Spiritual Prefect concerning the use of knowledge received by reason of their offices.

---

[11] Noldin-Schmitt, *Summa Theologiae Moralis* (3 vols., Oeniponte: Typis et Sumptibus Fel. Rauch, 1938–1940), II (25. ed., 1938), n. 666. Hereafter cited as *Summa Theologiae Moralis*.

[12] Noldin, *Summa Theologiae Moralis*, II, n. 669.

[13] Aertnys-Damen, *Theologia Moralis*, I, n. 1004.

[14] Merkelbach, *Summa Theologiae Moralis*, II, n. 855.

[15] Noldin-Schmitt, *Summa Theologiae Moralis*, II, 670.

B. ORDINARY CASES

If the clerical religious students approach the Spiritual Prefect to manifest the state of their souls to him, he is obliged by reason of this confidence to use the necessary care to respect that confidence, and to withhold from others all knowledge thus obtained. His revelation of knowledge gathered from a secret interview with a religious would cause distrust of him in the confidant, and a diminution of respect for his office. Consequently the Spiritual Prefect has an obligation to act with great prudence lest by his words, actions or omissions he should in any way impeach himself as unworthy of the public confidence placed in him. He cannot reveal to the Superiors the moral defects and the secret inclinations of others, so that those in charge of the community may give assignments which will remove each religious from dangers particular to him. The common good demands that he respect information confidentially given to him; otherwise both he and his office will fall into disrepute.

C. EXTRAORDINARY CASES

Suppose, however, these two extraordinary cases. The first concerns a religious whose presence constitutes a danger to the community because of his bad influence on a small group. The second case is that in which a religious is entirely unworthy for final profession and the reception of orders. In both cases the facts stated are acceptable as certainly true, the knowledge of them is possessed by the Spiritual Prefect only from a manifestation of conscience, and the Superiors who are altogether ignorant of the facts are making plans to advance the religious to orders. May the Spiritual Prefect reveal the offenses and the persons to the Superior in order to prevent grave harm to the community and the Church?

Even in these two extraordinary cases the Spiritual Prefect is bound to observe the confidence of the religious students, for he would cause greater harm to the Church by the disclosure of the transgressions than if he remained silent and watched unworthy candidates advance to the priesthood. It is true that an evil would be prevented by a word to the Superior, but a revelation of such a matter is soon recognized or suspected by others, and sometimes the fact of disclosure becomes even generally known, with the result that the Spiritual Prefect would bring down opprobium upon himself and his office, and the succeeding classes of religious students for many years would choose to keep their problems to themselves. As a consequence many would not receive the direction and the solution of spiritual difficulties which otherwise they would have received. Then again the matter revealed in the manifestation of conscience is something so sacred to the individual that he revolts at the thought of disclosing his spiritual life to another unless he has the fullest assurance that absolute secrecy will be observed. Never would the disclosure be made if even the least suspicion existed of its future revelation. A failure to observe this secrecy under all circumstances would have far-reaching ill effects in the life of a religious institute.

Pius XI, in the encyclical letter *Ad catholici sacerdotii* of December 20, 1935,[16] has this to say of the sacredness of the offices of confessor and spiritual director in the seminary:

> "Let Superiors of seminaries, together with the spiritual directors and confessors, reflect how weighty a responsibility they assume before God, before the Church, and before the youths themselves, if they do not take all means at their disposal to avoid a false step. We declare, too, that confessors and spiritual directors could also be responsible for such a grave error; not indeed because they can take any *outward action,* since that is severely forbidden them by their most delicate office itself, and often also by the inviolable sacramental seal; but because they can have a great influence on the souls of the individual students, and with paternal firmness they should guide each according to his spiritual needs. Should the superiors, for whatever cause, not take steps or show themselves weak, then especially should confessors and spiritual directors admonish the unsuited and unworthy, without any regard to human consideration, of their obligation to retire while yet there is time; . . ." [17]

In this encyclical Pius XI emphasizes the sacred character of

[16] *AAS,* XXVIII (1936), 5–53.

[17] *The Catholic Mind,* XXXIV (1936), Number 3, pp. 69, 70. Italics inserted by the writer.

the knowledge received either from confession or from the manifestation of conscience, and forbids the revelation even when it would prevent an unworthy candidate from proceeding to Orders.

Article IV. The Use of Knowledge Acquired by Observation

If the work of the Spiritual Prefect in an institute consists only in giving instructions to the students as a group and in offering exhortations, admonitions and corrections, he is able to use the information which he has gathered from an observation of the students in their daily monastic life. Matters which are of common knowledge in the community can be referred to in the instructions and admonitions without causing any suspicion that the Spiritual Prefect is breaking confidences.

If the Spiritual Prefect is the confessor of the religious clerics, he may use knowledge acquired from a source other than confession even though he receives the same knowledge in confession, provided that it is clear that he possesses, with certitude, knowledge from another source, and that he acts in this instance in view of his knowledge acquired through this other source. The knowledge obtained from the non-confessional source must, as has been said, be more than a matter of conjecture, or even of strong probability. It must be a matter of settled assurance and established certainty.[18] In the point here at issue great prudence must be observed. The same principles apply when the Spiritual Prefect knows with certainty from other sources what he learns in the manifestation of conscience.

Article V. The Use of Knowledge in Testimony Regarding the Students

In 1931 the Sacred Congregation of Religious issued an Instruction concerning the religious candidates for the priesthood and their training and testing before the reception of orders.[19] In this Instruction the Superiors of religious institutes are reminded of their obligation to allow no one to proceed to the re-

[18] Aertnys-Damen, *Theologia Moralis,* II, n. 462; Merkelbach, *Summa Theologiae Moralis,* III, n. 628.

[19] "*Quantum Religiones,*" 1 dec. 1931—*AAS,* XXIV (1932), 74–81.

ception of orders as long as they have not made sure, by means of a careful testing, of the candidate's moral character, piety, modesty, chastity, inclination for the clerical life, and progress in ecclesiastical studies and in religious discipline. In order the better to obtain this knowledge the Superiors are to consult the Spiritual Prefect and other persons, who by reason of their special acquaintance with the students know their life and ways.

In some communities external discipline is entrusted to the Spiritual Prefect. From his daily contact with the students in the external government of the house of studies, he is able to furnish valuable testimony to the Superiors. If he does not have authority in the external forum, but is limited to the work of instructing and exhorting the students, he may supply testimony to the Superiors from his observations of the students in their external observance of religious and monastic discipline. If he has received the confession of the students, he may reveal nothing whatsoever acquired from this source. The same prevails in regard to knowledge learned from the manifestation of conscience.[20] But even though he acts as a confessor and spiritual father, to whom the students make a manifestation of conscience, still the Spiritual Prefect may enlighten the Superiors concerning knowledge he has learned from sources other than confession and manifestation of conscience.[21]

Creusen [22] relates that in several instances the Holy See has authorized the Masters of novices to hear the confessions of the novices regularly. He states this fact in his commentary on the canon which requires that the Master of novices give a report to the Superior or the Chapter on the condition of the novices.[23] He does not say that the Master of novices in these cases is forbidden to give the report to the Superior or the Chapter. If such were the case, naturally one would expect him to state the fact. Hence, it is taken for granted that even in these cases the Master of novices is required to give a report to the proper authorities, despite the fact that he has received the confessions of the novices.

---

[20] Goyeneche, "Consultationes"—*CpRM*, XVIII (1937), 94, 95.

[21] *Supra*, p. 110.

[22] *Religious Men and Women in the Code*, n. 205.

[23] Canon 563.

If the Master of novices is permitted to proceed in this manner, so too may the Spiritual Prefect, provided that he limits himself to the use of knowledge which he has acquired with certitude from other sources than confession and manifestation of conscience.

Article VI. Voting on the Candidates for Profession and Orders

Canon 1361, § 3, prohibits the seeking of the vote of the confessor in a seminary when there is a question of his penitent's admission to orders or his dismissal from the seminary. Berutti [24] says that this prohibition is enacted for the sake of preserving the greatest liberty of conscience, lest there arise any impediments to the worthy reception of the sacrament of Penance by the students. Anxiety of conscience, too, is forestalled on the part of the confessor who may be aware through knowledge obtained outside the confessional that a candidate is unworthy, but nevertheless fears to vote according to his knowledge, lest he be suspected of violating the sacramental seal. A similar reason is present in the religious institute, and hence the vote of the confessor should not be sought. Beste [25] gives as his opinion that the vote of the Spiritual Prefect should not be sought in the case in which a vote is taken regarding the dismissal of a religious, if the former acts as confessor for the religious. This seems to be the only safe mode of procedure. It applies not only to the question of dismissal, but also to that of admittance to the sacrament of orders.

The prohibition against voting as binding the priest who receives the manifestation of conscience is not so strict. The rigid prohibition exists rather in regard to the revelation of secret knowledge. Such knowledge cannot be used to the detriment of the subject.[26] Goyeneche [27] says that the Spiritual Prefect is not permitted to use the secret knowledge which he has acquired from a manifestation of conscience when with others he takes

---

[24] *Institutiones,* IV, n. 124.
[25] *Commentarium in Codicem,* p. 400.
[26] Vermeersch, *De Religiosis,* n. 489.
[27] "Consultationes"—*CpRM,* XVIII (1937), 94, 95.

part in an election which decides whether the religious is to be admitted to final religious profession or to the reception of orders. Thus, in his opinion, the restriction in the matter of voting relative to the one who has received a manifestation of conscience affects only the use of the secret knowledge for making a decision against the candidate, and not the exercise of the vote as such. Since the revelation of conscience is made for the profit of the individual, the reposed confidence may not be betrayed. Thus, while there is a prohibition against the use of secret knowledge to the detriment of the candidate, there is no prohibition against the casting of a vote which relates to the future status of the religious.

CHAPTER IX

ADMONITIONS, INSTRUCTIONS AND EXHORTATIONS

Article I. Nature of These Duties

Canon 588, § 1, requires that the Spiritual Prefect form the souls of the religious clerical students by means of appropriate admonitions, instructions and exhortations.[1]

A. ADMONITIONS

The Latin word used to express admonition is "*monitis,*" which has the same common root as "*monitio.*" This latter term occurs in relation to the dismissal of religious and the application of penal remedies.[2] Canon 2307 states that the Ordinary either personally or through another is required to issue a warning when a person is in the proximate danger of committing a delict, or is gravely suspected of committing one. This points to a *canonical* admonition. It is an act of the Superior calling upon his subject to avoid an occasion of committing an offense or to change something in his character which is at least exteriorly reprehensible. It is administered in the nature of a caution and fatherly warning.[3]

An admonition in the sense implied in canon 588, § 1, is not a *canonical* admonition. It has as its purpose the advancement of the spiritual good of the individual religious. It seeks to accomplish this by indicating certain measures to be taken or avoided. It is an act by which the Spiritual Prefect emphasizes obligations already imposed, difficulties to be encountered, and dangers to be avoided, so that the students will be on their guard against the impediments to their spiritual progress. It is not simply of the

[1] ". . . opportunis monitis, instructionibus atque exhortationibus."

[2] E. g., canons 647, § 2, 2º; 649; 656, 2º; 658, § 1; 659; 660; 661, §§ 1, 3; 662; 663; 664, § 2; 2306, 1º; 2307; 2309, § 1; 2310.

[3] Ayrinhac, *Penal Legislation in the New Code of Canon Law* (New York, Cincinnati, Chicago: Benziger Brothers, 1920), n. 180.

negative character of a warning; it is rather of a positive character, inspired with advice and counsel.

B. INSTRUCTIONS

An *instruction* is an act by which a person explains a matter to another without necessarily using any influence to obtain further action. Its primary purpose is to educate the mind to things previously unknown.[4] The instruction given by the Spiritual Prefect should include a presentation of the truths necessary for salvation as well as of the considerations which serve for the religious and clerical perfection of the students. Since the instructions are to be imparted during the entire time devoted to studies, they should be accommodated to the grasp of the student. Hence they should follow a gradual progression in depth of content from the time immediately after the novitiate to that of ordination.

C. EXHORTATIONS

An *exhortation* bears a resemblance to an admonition inasmuch as both are concerned with arousing action in the listeners. An exhortation is an act by which a man, presupposing knowledge in another, strives to incite or arouse him to pursue that which he knows and believes. The Spiritual Prefect uses an exhortation when, by recalling the highest ideals and motives to the students, he urges them to strive for greater perfection. An exhortation seems of its very essence to be rather in the nature of an encouragement to good than of a warning against evil.

Admonitions, instructions and exhortations can be simultaneously present in the same sermon. By an instruction a teacher may clearly explain the truths of faith and morals, then follow the explanation with an exhortation to further action, and eventually conclude with an admonition to guard against certain dangers. Thus a preacher may instruct the people in regard to the duty of charity to one's neighbor, and follow the instruction with an exhortation to begin immediately practising the virtue, while at the

---

[4] Jansen, *Canonical Provisions for Catechetical Instruction,* The Catholic University of America Canon Law Studies, n. 107 (Washington, D. C.: The Catholic University of America Press, 1937), p. 3; Vermeersch-Creusen, *Epitome,* II, n. 664.

same time warn of the difficulties to be encountered in being charitable to enemies. Canon 588, § 1, requires that the admonitions, instructions and exhortations be appropriate, that is, they should be proportioned to the end that is to be obtained. The subject matter of the instructions remains to be considered and will be studied in the immediately subsequent article.

Article II. Subject Matter of These Functions

In order to determine the nature of the subject matter of the instructions given by the Spiritual Prefect to the students, it is necessary to know the purpose of these instructions. Canon 588, § 1, says that the Spiritual Prefect trains the souls of the students in the religious life. Immediately the question arises whether the phrase "*ad vitam religiosam*" refers only to the training of the students in the *religious* life, or whether it also includes the training of the religious clerics for the *sacerdotal* life.

In a lay religious institute the religious are not destined for the sacerdotal state, and therefore are not trained in the same manner as clerics. But in clerical religious institutes the religious clerics must be taught and disciplined both in the practices of the religious community and in the duties inherent in the sacerdotal office. Canon 588, § 1, specifically mentions the religious life, but not the clerical life—"*ad vitam religiosam*"—and therefore it might be concluded by some that the Spiritual Prefect is obliged by reason of this canon to train the souls of the clerics only in the religious life, and not in the clerical life. Thus, while the students would have the obligation to strive after religious and clerical perfection, the Spiritual Prefect by reason of the law would be bound only to advance the religious life of the individual.

The Sacred Congregation of Religious issued an Instruction on December 1, 1931,[5] by means of which it removed all difficulty on this point. The Congregation enumerated in detail the duties of the Spiritual Prefect. It specifically designated the clerical life along with the religious life as a matter whose proper formation and development await their actualization in the hands of the Spiritual Prefect.[6] In this Instruction it is stated that the training

[5] *AAS,* XXIV (1932), 74-81.

[6] ". . . ad vitam religiosam et clericalem . . ."—*AAS,* XXIV (1932), 77.

extends to both the clerical and the religious life. The purpose, then, of the instructions given by the Spiritual Prefect is to train the souls of the clerics in both the religious and the clerical life, to make them not only good religious but also good priests.

Knowing that the purpose of the training given by the Spiritual Prefect extends to both the religious and the clerical life, one may enunciate the principle that all truths necessary and useful for the accomplishment of this purpose may be made the subject matter of the instructions, admonitions and exhortations. The Spiritual Prefect, knowing the purpose of his work, will be able to discover endless material for his instructions and for the lessons to be drawn therefrom. He has at his disposal the whole of theology—dogmatic, moral, ascetical and mystical—as well as the Sacred Scriptures, the lives of the Saints, and the exemplary practices of holy men of his institute. To point out in greater detail the material which is made available through these sources is beyond the scope of this work.

However, it must be remembered that divine natural and divine positive law is determined in its more particular applications by ecclesiastical authority. Ecclesiastical laws, if considered in this sense, not only impose an obligation on the subject, but also make for his sanctification, and play an important part in his acquisition of good habits. These laws as they apply in a special manner to clerical religious students can profitably become a subject matter of the instructions given by the Spiritual Prefect.

The following topics are given as examples of ecclesiastical laws available as a basis of his instructions: the rights and privileges of clerics,[7] the obligations of clerics,[8] the obligations of religious,[9] confession and manifestation of conscience,[10] reverence for all the Sacraments,[11] preparation before and thanksgiving after mass,[12] the requisites in a subject for the sacrament of Orders,[13] duties in regard to the reservation of the Blessed Sacra-

[7] Canons 118–123.

[8] Canons 124–144.

[9] Canons 592–612.

[10] Canons 518, 519, 530.

[11] Canon 731, § 1.

[12] Canon 810.

[13] Canons 973–982.

ment.[14] Moreover, there are important documents issued by the Holy See which in a very special manner concern religious clerics. The four most important, which contain much appropriate material for the imparting of instruction, are the exhortation *Haerent animo* of Pius X,[15] wherein the Holy Father sets forth the sublimity of the sacerdotal vocation; the encyclical letter *Unigenitus Dei Filius* of Pius XI,[16] in which the training of religious both spiritually and intellectually is explained; the Instruction of December 1, 1931,[17] in which the norms for the testing and training of candidates for the priesthood in religious institutes are given; and finally the encyclical letter *Ad Catholici sacerdotii,*[18] in which Pope Pius XI gives a series of solid instructions and forceful exhortations on the nature, dignity, and destiny of the priesthood.

[14] Canons 1269–1272.

[15] 4 aug. 1908—*Fontes,* n. 683.

[16] March 19, 1924—*AAS,* XVI (1924), 133–148.

[17] *AAS,* XXIV (1932), 74–81.

[18] December 20, 1935—*AAS,* XXVIII (1936), 5–53.

CONCLUSIONS

The following opinions are offered as a summary of the preceding study:

1. The priest in charge of the students in houses of Regulars possessed disciplinary power over them in the period from Clement VIII (1603) to the enactment of the Code.

2. It cannot be proved from canon 588, or from the nature of the constitution of houses of study, that the Spiritual Prefect has authority in disciplinary matters under the present law.

3. It is in harmony with the practice of the Church for the Spiritual Prefect to have charge of the external discipline of the students together with the duty of their spiritual formation.

4. The silence of the present law concerning the external discipline of the students makes allowance for the customs and particular law of each institute.

5. The text of canon 588, § 2, does not contain a typographical error.

6. The qualities required for the Spiritual Prefect are the same moral qualities which are required for the Master of novices, the same physical qualities which are required for the Assistant Master.

7. The word "*oportet*" implies a real obligation. A probable opinion allows the Superior to choose a religious to act as Spiritual Prefect when he does not possess all the requirements of canon 588, § 2, provided that the religious has all the qualities which are demanded by the law of nature, and the Superior has only a few available candidates from which to make a choice.

8. The Spiritual Prefect who has no authority in the external forum may hear the confessions of the students, and may urge that a manifestation of conscience be made to him.

9. The Spiritual Prefect who has authority in the external forum may not hear the confessions of the students, but may urge that a manifestation of conscience be made to him.

10. The Spiritual Prefect may never reveal knowledge received through a confession or in a manifestation of conscience.

11. The Spiritual Prefect who hears the confessions of the students habitually should not vote on those students whenever it is a case of admission to religious profession, promotion to the reception of orders, and dismissal from the religious institute.

BIBLIOGRAPHY

SOURCES

Acta Apostolicae Sedis, Commentarium Officiale, Romae, 1909–

Acta Sanctae Sedis, 41 vols., Romae, 1865–1908.

Bullarum Diplomatum et Privilegiorum Sanctorum Romanorum Pontificum Taurinensis Editio, 25 vols., Augustae Taurinorum, 1857–1872.

Codex Iuris Canonici, Pii X Pontificis Maximi iussu digestus Benedicti Papae XV auctoritate promulgatus, ed. Petri Card. Gasparri, Civitate Vaticana: Typis Polyglottis Vaticanis, 1917.

Codicis Iuris Canonici Fontes cura Emi Petri Gasparri editi, 9 vols., Romae (postea Civitate Vaticana): Typis Polyglottis Vaticanis, 1923–1939, Vols. VII, VIII, IX, ed. cura et studio Emi Iustiniani Card. Serédi.

Constitutiones Fratrum S. Ordinis Praedicatorum, ed. nova, Parisiis, 1886.

Constitutiones Ordinis Beatissimae Virginis Mariae de Monte Carmelo, Typis Polyglottis Vaticanis, 1930.

Constitutiones Ordinis Fratrum Minorum Sancti Patris Francisci Conventualium, Romae: Ad SS. XII Apostolos, 1932.

Constitutiones Piae Societatis Missionum, Ratisbonae: Pustet, post 1922.

Corpus Iuris Canonici, Editio Lipsiensis 2., 2 vols., Richter-Friedberg, Lipsiae, 1879–1881.

Harduinus, Ioannes, *Acta Conciliorum et Epistolae Decretales ac Constitutiones Summorum Pontificum,* ed. Regia, 12 vols., Parisiis, 1715.

Jaffé, Philippus, *Regesta Pontificum Romanorum ab condita Ecclesia ad annum post Christum natum MCXCVIII,* 2. ed., correctam et auctam auspiciis Gulielmi Wattenbach curaverunt S. Loewenfeld, F. Kaltenbrunner, P. Ewald, 2 vols. in 1, Lipsiae, 1885–1888.

Mansi, J. D., *Sacrorum Conciliorum Nova et Amplissima Collectio,* 53 vols. in 60, Paris, Leipzig, Arnhem, 1901–1927.

Potthast, Augustus, *Regesta Pontificum Romanorum inde ab anno post Christum natum MCXCVIII ad annum MCCCIV,* 2 vols., Berolini, 1874–1875.

Regulae et Constitutiones Congregationis Sancti Spiritus sub tutela Immaculati Cordis Beatissimae Virginis Mariae, Norwalk, Conn., 1934.

Regula Primitiva et Constitutiones Fratrum Discalceatorum Ordinis Sanctissimae Trinitatis Redemptionis Captivorum, Isola del Liri: Soc. Tip. A. Macioce & Pisani, 1933.

The Constitutions of the Oblates of Saint Francis De Sales, Translation published by the American Province, 1929.

The Rules and General Constitutions of the Friars Minor, Paterson, N. J.: St. Anthony Guild Press, 1936.

AUTHORS

Aertnys, J.-Damen, C., *Theologia Moralis secundum Doctrinam S. Alfonsi De Ligorio Doct. Ecclesiae,* 2 vols., 13. ed., Taurini-Romae: Marietti, 1939.

Ayrinhac, H. A., *Penal Legislation in the New Code of Canon Law,* New York, Cincinnati, Chicago: Benziger Brothers, 1920.

Bachofen, Charles Augustine, *Compendium Iuris Regularium,* New York, 1903.

(Bachofen), Charles Augustine, *A Commentary on the New Code of Canon Law,* 8 vols., St. Louis: B. Herder Book Co.

Bastien, Pierre, *Directoire Canonique,* Maredsous, 1904.

Berutti, Christophorus, *Institutiones Iuris Canonici,* 6 vols., Taurini-Romae: Marietti, Vol. III, 1936; Vol. IV, 1940.

Beste, Udalricus, *Introductio in Codicem,* 2. ed., Collegeville, Minn.: St. John's Abbey Press, 1944.

Butler, Cuthbert, *Benedictine Monachism,* London: Longmans, Green and Co., 1919.

———, *Lausiac History of Palladius,* Cambridge, 1898.

———, *Sancti Benedicti Regula Monasteriorum, Editio Critico-Practica,* 2. ed., Friburgi Brisgoviae: Herder, 1927.

Cance, Adrien, *Le Code de Droit Canonique,* 3 vols., Paris: J. Gabalda et Fils, Vol. II, 6. ed., 1930.

Cappello, Felix, *Summa Iuris Canonici in Usum Scholarum Concinnata,* 3 vols., Vol. II, 3. ed., 1939, Romae, apud Aedes Universitatis Gregorianae.

———, *Tractatus Canonico—Moralis de Sacramentis,* 2 vols., Vol. II, par. 1, 2. ed., Romae: Marietti, 1928.

Chelodi, Ioannes, *Ius de Personis iuxta Codicem Iuris Canonici,* ed. altera a Sac. Ernesto Bertagnolli recognita et aucta, Tridenti: Libr. Edit. Tridentum, 1927.

Clancy, Patrick, *The Local Religious Superior,* The Catholic University of America Canon Law Studies, n. 175, Washington, D. C.: The Catholic University of America Press, 1943.

Cocchi, Guidus, *Commentarium in Codicem Iuris Canonici,* 8 vols., Taurinorum Augustae: Marietti, Vol. III, 4. ed., 1940; Vol. VI, 3. ed., 1932.

Coronata, Matthaeus Conte a, *Institutiones Iuris Canonici ad Usum Utriusque Cleri et Scholarum,* 5 vols., Taurini (Italia): Marietti, 1928–1936.

Creusen, Joseph-Ellis, Adam C.,-Garesche, Edward F., *Religious Men and Women in the Code,* 4. ed., Milwaukee: Bruce, 1940.

Dube, Arthur, *The General Principles for the Reckoning of Time in Canon Law,* The Catholic University of America Canon Law Studies, No. 144, Washington, D. C.: The Catholic University of America Press, 1941.

Fanfani, Ludovicus, *De Iure Religiosorum ad Normam Codicis Iuris Canonici,* 2. ed., Taurini-Romae: Marietti, 1925.

Ferreres, Ioannes, *Institutiones Canonicae,* 2. ed., 2 vols., Barcinonae, 1920.

Jansen, Raymond, *Canonical Provisions for Catechetical Instruction,* The Catholic University of America Canon Law Studies, n. 107, Washington, D. C.: The Catholic University of America Press, 1937.

Leurenius, Petrus, *Forum Beneficiale,* Venetiis, 1742.

Maroto, Philippus, *Institutiones Iuris Canonici ad Normam Novi Codicis,* 2 vols., Vol. I, Matriti, 1919.

Merkelbach, Benedictus, *Summa Theologiae Moralis ad Mentem D. Thomae et ad Normam Iuris Canonici,* 3 vols., Vol. II, 3. ed., 1938; Vol. III, 2. ed., 1936, Parisiis: Desclée de Brouwer et Soc.

Migne, J. P., *Patrologiae Cursus Completus,* Series Latina, 221 vols., Parisiis, 1844–1855;—Series Graeca, 161 vols., Parisiis, 1857–1866.

Noldin, H.–Schmitt, A., *Summa Theologiae Moralis,* 3 vols., Oeniponte: Typis et Sumptibus Fel. Rauch, 1938–1940, Vol. II, 25. ed., 1938.

Ottaviani, Alaphridus, *Institutiones Iura Publici Ecclesiastici,* 2. ed., 2 vols., Civitate Vaticana: Typis Polyglottis Vaticanis, 1935–1936.

Piatus, Montensis, *Praelectiones Iuris Regularium,* 2 vols., Tornaci, 1888.

Pejška, Josephus, *Ius Canonicum Religiosorum,* 3. ed., Friburgi Brisgoviae: Herder, 1927.

Prümmer, Dominicus, *Manuale Iuris Ecclesiastici,* 3. ed., Friburgi Brisgoviae, Herder, 1922.

Raus, I. B., *Institutiones Canonicae iuxta Novum Codicem Iuris pro scholis vel ad usum privatum syntheticae redactae,* 2. ed., Lugduni: Vitte, 1931.

———, *De Sacrae Obedientiae Virtute et Voto secundum Doctrinam Divi Thomae et S. Alphonsi, iuxta Normas ac Codicem Iuris Canonici,* 2 vols. in 1, Lugduni, Lutetiae Parisiorum: apud Emmanuelam Vitte, 1923.

Raymond of Pennafort, *Summa de Casibus,* ed. nova, Verona, 1744.

Reiffenstuel, Anacletus, *Jus Canonicum Universum,* 5 vols. in 7, Parisiis, 1864–1870.

Schaefer, Timotheus, *De Religiosis ad Normam Codicis Iuris Canonici,* 3. ed., Romae, 1940.

Shuhler, Ralph, *Privileges of Regulars to Absolve and Dispense,* The Catholic University of America Canon Law Studies, n. 186, Washington, D. C.: The Catholic University of America Press, 1943.

Sipos, Stephanus, *Enchiridion Iuris Canonici,* 3. ed., Pécs: Ex Typographia "Haladas R. T.," 1936.

Suarez, Franciscus, *Opera Omnia,* ed. nova, 28 vols., Vols. I-IV a D. M. André; Vols. V-XXVI a Carolo Berton, Parisiis, 1856–1878.

Toso, Albertus, *Ad Codicem Iuris Canonici Commentaria Minora,* 5 vols., Vol. V, Romae, 1927.

Vermeersch, A., *De Religiosis Institutis et Personis*, 2 vols., Brugis, Romae et Ratisbonae, Lutetiae Parisiorum, 1909.

Vermeersch, A.-Creusen, J., *Epitome Iuris Canonici cum Commentariis ad Scholas et ad Usum Privatum*, 3 vols., Vol. 1, 6. ed., 1937, Vol. II, 6. ed., 1940, Mechliniae-Romae: Dessain.

Wernz, Franciscus, *Ius Decretalium*, 6 vols., Romae et Prati, 1898–1905.

Wernz, F.-Vidal, P., *Ius Canonicum ad Codicis Normam exactum*, 7 vols. in 8, Romae: apud Aedes Universitatis Gregorianae, 1923–1938, Vol. II, 2. ed., 1928, Vol. III, 1933.

ARTICLES

Blat, Albertus, "De Potestate Superiorum in Religionibus secundum Codicem I. C."—*CpRM*, XVI (1935), 321–353.

Boudinhon, "An nullus semper sit actus Superioris non petito consilio?"—*JP*, VIII (1928), 29–35.

Canuto, A., "De regimine domus studiorum in religione clericali exempta ad normam can. 588"—*Apollinaris*, IX (1936), 19–39.

Goyeneche, S., "Consultationes"—*CpR*, I (1920), 140–145; V (1924), 154–166; VII (1926), 183–190; IX (1928), 115–119; *CpRM*, XVIII (1937), 94, 95.

Langasco, Agathangelus a, "De Natura Juridica et Regimine Scholarum Internarum Religiosorum"—*JP*, XVI (1936), 165–181.

———, "De regimine domus studiorum in religione clericali"—*JP*, XVIII (1938), 118–131; XIX (1939), 55–69, 191–201.

Larraona, Arcadius, "Consultationes"—*CpR*, I (1920), 51–57.

———, "Commentarium Codicis"—*CpR*, X (1929), 250–259; XII (1931), 119–130.

Oesterle, Gerardus, "De ratione studiorum in religionibus clericalibus"—*CpR*, VI (1925), 296–323.

Saucedo, P., "Exercitium jurisdictionis et superiores laici ex Ordine Hospitalario S. Joannis de Deo"—*CpR*, XIII (1932), 51–61; 106–114; 224–231; 291–302.

Van de Kerckhove, M., "De notione jurisdictionis in iure romano"—*JP*, XVI (1936), 49–65.

———, "De notione jurisdictionis apud Decretistas et Priores Decretalistas"—*JP*, XVIII (1938), 10–14.

Vermeersch, A., "De unitate confessarii ordinarii apud Moniales et Sorores"—*Periodica de Re Canonica et Morali utili praesertim Religiosis et Missionariis*, V (1913), (1)–(12).

Voltas, Petrus, "De aperienda, directionis causa, Superioribus conscientia"—*CpR*, I (1920), 83–92, 117–125, 145–151.

PERIODICALS

Apollinaris, Romae, 1928–

Commentarium pro Religiosis, Romae, 1920–; ab anno 1935; *Commentarium pro Religiosis et Missionariis.*

Ius Pontificium, Romae, 1921–

Periodica de Re Canonica et Morali utili praesertim Religiosis et Missionariis, Bruges, 1905–

ABBREVIATIONS

AAS—*Acta Apostolicae Sedis.*

Bull. Rom. Taur.—*Bullarum Diplomatum et Privilegiorum Romanorum Pontificum Taurinensis Editio.*

CpR—*Commentarium pro Religiosis.*

CpRM—*Commentarium pro Religiosis et Missionariis.*

D.—Digestum (Iustinianum).

Fontes—*Codicis Iuris Canonici Fontes cura . . . Gasparri editi.*

J (K-E-L)—Jaffe (Kaltenbrunner, Ewald, Loewenfeld).

JP—*Ius Pontificium.*

Mansi—*Sacrorum Conciliorum Nova et Amplissima Collectio.*

MPL—Migne, *Patrologia Latina.*

MPG—Migne, *Patrologia Graeca.*

N.—Novellae (Iustinianae).

S.C.C.—Sacra Congregatio Concilii.

S.C. Ep. et Reg.—Sacra Congregatio Episcoporum et Regularium.

S.C.S. Off.—Sacra Congregatio Sancti Officii.

ALPHABETICAL INDEX

BIOGRAPHICAL NOTE

Nicholas Gill was born on June 3, 1913, at Wilkes-Barre, Pa. After completing his elementary and high school studies in the schools of that city, he entered St. Thomas College at Scranton in 1930. He was admitted to the Passionist Novitiate in 1932 and made his religious profession on August 15, 1933. He was ordained to the priesthood on April 23, 1940. In the autumn of 1942 he entered the School of Canon Law of the Catholic University of America, where he received the degree of the Baccalaureate in Canon Law in May, 1943, and the degree of the Licentiate in Canon Law in May, 1944.

CANON LAW STUDIES*

1. FRERIKS, REV. CELESTINE A., C.PP.S., J.C.D., Religious Congregations in Their External Relations, 121 pp., 1916.
2. GALLIHER, REV. DANIEL M., O.P., J.C.D., Canonical Elections, 117 pp., 1917.
3. BORKOWSKI, REV. AURELIUS L., O.F.M., J.C.D., De Confraternitatibus Ecclesiasticis, 136 pp., 1918.
4. CASTILLO, REV. CAYO, J.C.D., Disertacion Historico-Canonica sobre la Potestad del Cabildo en Sede Vacante o Impedida del Vicario Capitular, 99 pp., 1919 (1918).
5. KUBELBECK, REV. WILLIAM J., S.T.B., J.C.D., The Sacred Penitentiaria and Its Relation to Faculties of Ordinaries and Priests, 129 pp., 1918.
6. PETROVITS, REV. JOSEPH J. C., S.T.D., J.C.D., The New Church Law on Matrimony, X-461 pp., 1919.
7. HICKEY, REV. JOHN J., S.T.B., J.C.D., Irregularities and Simple Impediments in the New Code of Canon Law, 100 pp., 1920.
8. KLEKOTKA, REV. PETER J., S.T.B., J.C.D., Diocesan Consultors, 179 pp., 1920.
9. WANENMACHER, REV. FRANCIS, J.C.D., The Evidence in Ecclesiastical Procedure Affecting the Marriage Bond, 1920 (Printed 1935).
10. GOLDEN, REV. HENRY FRANCIS, J.C.D., Parochial Benefices in the New Code, IV-119 pp., 1921 (Printed 1925).
11. KOUDELKA, REV. CHARLES J., J.C.D., Pastors, Their Rights and Duties According to the New Code of Canon Law, 211 pp., 1921.
12. MELO, REV. ANTONIUS, O.F.M., J.C.D., De Exemptione Regularium, X-188 pp., 1921.
13. SCHAAF, REV. VALENTINE THEODORE, O.F.M., S.T.B., J.C.D., The Cloister, X-180 pp., 1921.
14. BURKE, REV. THOMAS JOSEPH, S.T.D., J.C.D., Competence in Ecclesiastical Tribunals, IV-117 pp., 1922.
15. LEECH, REV. GEORGE LEO, J.C.D., A Comparative Study of the Constitution "Apostolicae Sedis" and the "Codex Juris Canonici," 179 pp., 1922.
16. MOTRY, REV. HUBERT LOUIS, S.T.D., J.C.D., Diocesan Faculties According to the Code of Canon Law, II-167 pp., 1922.
17. MURPHY, REV. GEORGE LAWRENCE, J.C.D., Delinquencies and Penalties in the Administration and the Reception of the Sacraments, IV-121 pp., 1923.

* Below n. 100 only numbers 25 and 57 are still available. Beginning with n. 100 only the following numbers are unavailable: Nos. 100–118 inclusive, and also n. 122.

18. O'Reilly, Rev. John Anthony, S.T.B., J.C.D., Ecclesiastical Sepulture in the New Code of Canon Law, II-129 pp., 1923.
19. Michalicka, Rev. Wenceslas Cyrill, O.S.B., J.C.D., Judicial Procedure in Dismissal of Clerical Exempt Religious, 107 pp., 1923.
20. Dargin, Rev. Edward Vincent, S.T.B., J.C.D., Reserved Cases According to the Code of Canon Law, IV-103 pp., 1924.
21. Godfrey, Rev. John A., S.T.B., J.C.D., The Right of Patronage According to the Code of Canon Law, 153 pp., 1924.
22. Hagedorn, Rev. Francis Edward, J.C.D., General Legislation on Indulgences, II-154 pp., 1924.
23. King, Rev. James Ignatius, J.C.D., The Administration of the Sacraments to Dying Non-Catholics, V-141 pp., 1924.
24. Winslow, Rev. Francis Joseph, O.F.M., J.C.D., Vicars and Prefects Apostolic, IV-149 pp., 1924.
25. Correa, Rev. Jose Servelion, S.T.L., J.C.D., La Potestad Legislativa de la Iglesia Catolica, IV-127 pp., 1925.
26. Dugan, Rev. Henry Francis, A.M., J.C.D., The Judiciary Department of the Diocesan Curia, 87 pp., 1925.
27. Keller, Rev. Charles Frederick, S.T.B., J.C.D., Mass Stipends, 167 pp., 1925.
28. Paschang, Rev. John Linus, J.C.D., The Sacramentals According to the Code of Canon Law, 129 pp., 1925.
29. Piontek, Rev. Cyrillus, O.F.M., S.T.B., J.C.D., De Indulto Exclaustrationis necnon Saecularizationis, XIII-289 pp., 1925.
30. Kearney, Rev. Richard Joseph, S.T.B., J.C.D., Sponsors at Baptism According to the Code of Canon Law, IV-127 pp., 1925.
31. Bartlett, Rev. Chester Joseph, A.M., LL.B., J.C.D., The Tenure of Parochial Property in the United States of America, V-108 pp., 1926.
32. Kilker, Rev. Adrian Jerome, J.C.D., Extreme Unction, V-425 pp., 1926.
33. McCormick, Rev. Robert Emmett, J.C.D., Confessors of Religious, VIII-266 pp., 1926.
34. Miller, Rev. Newton Thomas, J.C.D., Founded Masses According to the Code of Canon Law, VII-93 pp., 1926.
35. Roelker, Rev. Edward G., S.T.D., J.C.D., Principles of Privilege According to the Code of Canon Law, XI-166 pp., 1926.
36. Bakalarczyk, Rev. Richardus, M.I.C., J.U.D., De Novitiatu, VIII-208 pp., 1927.
37. Pizzuti, Rev. Lawrence, O.F.M., J.U.L., De Parochis Religiosis, 1927. (Not Printed.)
38. Bliley, Rev. Nicholas Martin, O.S.B., J.C.D., Altars According to the Code of Canon Law, XIX-132 pp., 1927.
39. Brown, Mr. Brendan Francis, A.B., LL.M., J.U.D., The Canonical Juristic Personality with Special Reference to its Status in the United States of America, V-212 pp., 1927.

40. CAVANAUGH, REV. WILLIAM THOMAS, C.P., J.U.D., The Reservation of the Blessed Sacrament, VIII-101 pp., 1927.
41. DOHENY, REV. WILLIAM J., C.S.C., A.B., J.U.D., Church Property: Modes of Acquisition, X-118 pp., 1927.
42. FELDHAUS, REV. ALOYSIUS H., C.PP.S., J.C.D., Oratories, IX-141 pp., 1927.
43. KELLY, REV. JAMES PATRICK, A.B., J.C.D., The Jurisdiction of the Simple Confessor, X-208 pp., 1927.
44. NEUBERGER, REV. NICHOLAS J., J.C.D., Canon 6 or the Relation of the Codex Juris Canonici to the Preceding Legislation, V-95 pp., 1927.
45. O'KEEFE, REV. GERALD MICHAEL, J.C.D., Matrimonial Dispensations, Powers of Bishops, Priests, and Confessors, VIII-232 pp., 1927.
46. QUIGLEY, REV. JOSEPH A. M., A.B., J.C.D., Condemned Societies, 139 pp., 1927.
47. ZAPLOTNIK, REV. JOHANNES LEO, J.C.D., De Vicariis Foraneis, X-142 pp., 1927.
48. DUSKIE, REV. JOHN ALOYSIUS, A.B., J.C.D., The Canonical Status of the Orientals in the United States, VIII-196 pp., 1928.
49. HYLAND, REV. FRANCIS EDWARD, J.C.D., Excommunication, Its Nature, Historical Development and Effects, VIII-181 pp., 1928.
50. REINMANN, REV. GERALD JOSEPH, O.M.C., J.C.D., The Third Order Secular of Saint Francis, 201 pp., 1928.
51. SCHENK, REV. FRANCIS J., J.C.D., The Matrimonial Impediments of Mixed Religion and Disparity of Cult, XVI-318 pp., 1929.
52. COADY, REV. JOHN JOSEPH, S.T.D., J.U.D., A.M., The Appointment of Pastors, VIII-150 pp., 1929.
53. KAY, REV. THOMAS HENRY, J.C.D., Competence in Matrimonial Procedure, VIII-164 pp., 1929.
54. TURNER, REV. SIDNEY JOSEPH, C.P., J.U.D., The Vow of Poverty, XLIX-217 pp., 1929.
55. KEARNEY, REV. RAYMOND A., A.B., S.T.D., J.C.D., The Principles of Delegation, VII-149 pp., 1929.
56. CONRAN, REV. EDWARD JAMES, A.B., J.C.D., The Interdict, V-163 pp., 1930.
57. O'NEILL, REV. WILLIAM H., J.C.D., Papal Rescripts of Favor, VII-218 pp., 1930.
58. BASTNAGEL, REV. CLEMENT VINCENT, J.U.D., The Appointment of Parochial Adjutants and Assistants, XV-257 pp., 1930.
59. FERRY, REV. WILLIAM A., A.B., J.C.D., Stole Fees, V-136 pp., 1930.
60. COSTELLO, REV. JOHN MICHAEL, A.B., J.C.D., Domicile and Quasi-Domicile, VII-201 pp., 1930.
61. KREMER, REV. MICHAEL NICHOLAS, A.B., S.T.B., J.C.D., Church Support in the United States, VI-136 pp., 1930.
62. ANGULO, REV. LUIS, C.M., J.C.D., Legislation de la Iglesia sobre la intencion en la application de la Santa Misa, VII-104 pp., 1931.

63. FREY, REV. WOLFGANG NORBERT, O.S.B., A.B., J.C.D., The Act of Religious Profession, VIII-174 pp., 1931.
64. ROBERTS, REV. JAMES BRENDAN, A.B., J.C.D., The Banns of Marriage, XIV-140 pp., 1931.
65. RYDER, REV. RAYMOND ALOYSIUS, A.B., J.C.D., Simony, IX-151 pp., 1931.
66. CAMPAGNA, REV. ANGELO, PH.D., J.U.D., Il Vicario Generale del Vescovo, VII-205 pp., 1931.
67. COX, REV. JOSEPH GODFREY, A.B., J.C.D., The Administration of Seminaries, VI-124 pp., 1931.
68. GREGORY, REV. DONALD J., J.U.D., The Pauline Privilege, XV-165 pp., 1931.
69. DONOHUE, REV. JOHN F., J.C.D., The Impediment of Crime, VII-110 pp., 1931.
70. DOOLEY, REV. EUGENE A., O.M.I., J.C.D., Church Law on Sacred Relics, IX-143 pp., 1931.
71. ORTH, REV. CLEMENT RAYMOND, O.M.C., J.C.D., The Approbation of Religious Institutes, 171 pp., 1931.
72. PERNICONE, REV. JOSEPH M., A.B., J.C.D., The Ecclesiastical Prohibition of Books, XII-267 pp., 1932.
73. CLINTON, REV. CONNELL, A.B., J.C.D., The Paschal Precept, IX-108 pp., 1932.
74. DONNELLY, REV. FRANCIS B., A.M., S.T.L., J.C.D., The Diocesan Synod, VIII-125 pp., 1932.
75. TORRENTE, REV. CAMILO, C.M.F., J.C.D., Las Procesiones Sagradas, V-145 pp., 1932.
76. MURPHY, REV. EDWIN J., C.PP.S., J.C.D., Suspension Ex Informata Conscientia, XI-122 pp., 1932.
77. MACKENZIE, REV. ERIC F., A.M., S.T.L., J.C.D., The Delict of Heresy in its Commission, Penalization, Absolution, VII-124 pp., 1932.
78. LYONS, REV. AVITUS E., S.T.B., J.C.D., The Collegiate Tribunal of First Instance, XI-147 pp., 1932.
79. CONNOLLY, REV. THOMAS A., J.C.D., Appeals, XI-195 pp., 1932.
80. SANGMEISTER, REV. JOSEPH V., A.B., J.C.D., Force and Fear as Precluding Matrimonial Consent, V-211 pp., 1932.
81. JAEGER, REV. LEO A., A.B., J.C.D., The Administration of Vacant and Quasi-Vacant Episcopal Sees in the United States, IX-229 pp., 1932.
82. RIMLINGER, REV. HERBERT T., J.C.D., Error Invalidating Matrimonial Consent, VII-79 pp., 1932.
83. BARRETT, REV. JOHN D. M., S.S., J.C.D., A Comparative Study of the Third Plenary Council of Baltimore and the Code, IX-221 pp., 1932.
84. CARBERRY, REV. JOHN J., PH.D., S.T.D., J.C.D., The Juridical Form of Marriage, X-177 pp., 1934.
85. DOLAN, REV. JOHN L., A.B., J.C.D., The Defensor Vinculi, XII-157 pp., 1934.

86. HANNAN, REV. JEROME D., A.M., S.T.D., LL.B., J.C.D., The Canon Law of Wills, IX-517 pp., 1934.
87. LEMIEUX, REV. DELISE A., A.M., J.C.D., The Sentence in Ecclesiastical Procedure, IX-131 pp., 1934.
88. O'ROURKE, REV. JAMES J., A.B., J.C.D., Parish Registers, VII-109 pp., 1934.
89. TIMLIN, REV. BARTHOLOMEW, O.F.M., A.M., J.C.D., Conditional Matrimonial Consent, X-381 pp., 1934.
90. WAHL, REV. FRANCIS X., A.B., J.C.D., The Matrimonial Impediments of Consanguinity and Affinity, VI-125 pp., 1934.
91. WHITE, REV. ROBERT J., A.B., LL.B., S.T.B., J.C.D., Canonical Ante-Nuptial Promises and the Civil Law, VI-152 pp., 1934.
92. HERRERA, REV. ANTONIO PARRA, O.C.D., J.C.D., Legislacion Ecclesiastica sobra el Ayuno y la Abstinencia, XI-191 pp., 1935.
93. KENNEDY, REV. EDWIN J., J.C.D., The Special Matrimonial Process in Cases of Evident Nullity, X-165 pp., 1935.
94. MANNING, REV. JOHN J., A.B., J.C.D., Presumption of Law in Matrimonial Procedure, XI-111 pp., 1935.
95. MOEDER, REV. JOHN M., J.C.D., The Proper Bishop for Ordination and Dimissorial Letters, VII-135 pp., 1935.
96. O'MARA, REV. WILLIAM A., A.B., J.C.D., Canonical Causes for Matrimonial Dispensations, IX-155 pp., 1935.
97. 'REILLY, REV. PETER, J.C.D., Residence of Pastors, IX-81 pp., 1935.
98. SMITH, REV. MARINER T., O.P., S.T.Lr., J.C.D., The Penal Law for Religious, VII-169 pp., 1935.
99. WHALEN, REV. DONALD W., A.M., J.C.D., The Value of Testimonial Evidence in Matrimonial Procedure, XIII-297 pp., 1935.
100. CLEARY, REV. JOSEPH F., J.C.D., Canonical Limitations on the Alienation of Church Property, VIII-141 pp., 1936.
101. GLYNN, REV. JOHN C., J.C.D., The Promoter of Justice, XX-337 pp., 1936.
102. BRENNAN, REV. JAMES H., S.S., M.A., S.T.B., J.C.D., The Simple Convalidation of Marriage, VI-135 pp., 1937.
103. BRUNINI, REV. JOSEPH BERNARD, J.C.D., The Clerical Obligations of Canons 139 and 142, X-121 pp., 1937.
104. CONNOR, REV. MAURICE, A.B., J.C.D., The Administrative Removal of Pastors, VIII-159 pp., 1937.
105. GUILFOYLE, REV. MERLIN JOSEPH, J.C.D., Custom, XI-144 pp., 1937.
106. HUGHES, REV. JAMES AUSTIN, A.B., A.M., J.C.D., Witnesses in Criminal Trials of Clerics, IX-140 pp., 1937.
107. JANSEN, REV. RAYMOND J., A.B., S.T.L., J.C.D., Canonical Provisions for Catechetical Instruction, VII-153 pp., 1937.
108. KEALY, REV. JOHN JAMES, A.B., J.C.D., The Introductory Libellus in Church Court Procedure, XI-121 pp., 1937.

109. McManus, Rev. James Edward, C.SS.R., J.C.D., The Administration of Temporal Goods in Religious Institutes, XVI-196 pp., 1937.
110. Moriarty, Rev. Eugene James, J.C.D., Oaths in Ecclesiastical Courts, X-115 pp., 1937.
111. Rainer, Rev. Eligius George, C.SS.R., J.C.D., Suspension of Clerics, XVII-249 pp., 1937.
112. Reilly, Rev. Thomas F., C.SS.R., J.C.D., Visitation of Religious, VI-195 pp., 1938.
113. Moriarty, Rev. Francis E. C.SS.R., J.C.D., The Extraordinary Absolution from Censures, XV-334 pp., 1938.
114. Connolly, Rev. Nicholas P., J.C.D., The Canonical Erection of Parishes, X-132 pp., 1938.
115. Donovan, Rev. James Joseph, J.C.D., The Pastor's Obligation in Prenuptial Investigation, XII-322 pp., 1938.
116. Harrigan, Rev. Robert J., M.A., S.T.B., J.C.D., The Radical Sanation of Invalid Marriages, VIII-208 pp., 1938.
117. Boffa, Rev. Conrad Humbert, J.C.D., Canonical Provisions for Catholic Schools, VII-211 pp., 1939.
118. Parsons, Rev. Anscar John, O.M.Cap., J.C.D., Canonical Elections, XII-236 pp., 1939.
119. Reilly, Rev. Edward Michael, A.B., J.C.D., The General Norms of Dispensation, XII-156 pp., 1939.
120. Ryan, Rev. Gerald Aloysius, A.B., J.C.D., Principles of Episcopal Jurisdiction, XII-172 pp., 1939.
121. Burton, Rev. Francis James, C.S.C., A.B., J.C.D., A Commentary on Canon 1125, X-222 pp., 1940.
122. Miaskiewicz, Rev. Francis Sigismund, J.C.D., Supplied Jurisdiction According to Canon 209, XII-340 pp., 1940.
123. Rice, Rev. Patrick William, A.B., J.C.D., Proof of Death in Prenuptial Investigation, VIII-156 pp., 1940.
124. Anglin, Rev. Thomas Francis, M.S., J.C.D., The Eucharistic Fast, VIII-183 pp., 1941.
125. Coleman, Rev. John Jerome, J.C.D., The Minister of Confirmation, VI-153 pp., 1941.
126. Downs, Rev. Joseph Emmanuel, A.B., J.C.D., The Concept of Clerical Immunity, XI-163 pp., 1941.
127. Esswein, Rev. Anthony Albert, J.C.D., Extrajudicial Penal Powers of Ecclesiastical Superiors, X-144 pp., 1941.
128. Farrell, Rev. Benjamin Francis, M.A., S.T.L., J.C.D., The Rights and Duties of the Local Ordinary Regarding Congregations of Women Religious of Pontifical Approval, V-195 pp., 1941.
129. Feeney, Rev. Thomas John, A.B., S.T.L., J.C.D., Restitutio in Integrum, VI-169 pp., 1941.
130. Findlay, Rev. Stephen William, O.S.B., A.B., J.C.D., Canonical

Norms Governing the Deposition and Degradation of Clerics, XVII-279 pp., 1941.

131. Goodwine, Rev. John, A.B., S.T.L., J.C.D., The Right of the Church to Acquire Property, VIII-119 pp., 1941.
132. Heston, Rev. Edward Louis, C.S.C., Ph.D., S.T.D., J.C.D., The Alienation of Church Property in the United States, XII-222 pp., 1941.
133. Hogan, Rev. James John, A.B., S.T.L., J.C.D., Judicial Advocates and Procurators, XIII-200 pp., 1941.
134. Kealy, Rev. Thomas M., A.B., Litt.B., J.C.D., Dowry of Women Religious, IX-152 pp., 1941.
135. Keene, Rev. Michael James, O.S.B., J.C.D., Religious Ordinaries and Canon 198, V-164 pp., 1942.
136. Kerin, Rev. Charles A., S.S., M.A., S.T.B., J.C.D., The Privation of Christian Burial, XVI-279 pp., 1941.
137. Louis, Rev. William Francis, M.A., J.C.D., Diocesan Archives, X-101 pp., 1941.
138. McDevitt, Rev. Gilbert Joseph, A.B., J.C.D., Legitimacy and Legitimation, X-247 pp., 1941.
139. McDonough, Rev. Thomas Joseph, A.B., J.C.D., Apostolic Administrators, X-217 pp., 1941.
140. **Meier, Rev. Carl Anthony, A.B., J.C.D., Penal Administrative Pro**cedure Against Negligent Pastors, XI-240 pp., 1941.
141. Schmidt, Rev. John Rogg, A.B., J.C.D., The Principles of Authentic Interpretation in Canon 17 of the Code of Canon Law, XII-331 pp., 1941.
142. Slafkosky, Rev. Andrew Leonard, A.B., J.C.D., The Canonical Episcopal Visitation of the Diocese, X-197 pp., 1941.
143. Swoboda, Rev. Innocent Robert, O.F.M., J.C.D., Ignorance in Relation to the Imputability of Delicts, IX-271 pp., 1941.
144. Dubé, Rev. Arthur Joseph, A.B., J.C.D., The General Principles for the Reckoning of Time in Canon Law, VIII-299 pp., 1941.
145. McBride, Rev. James T., A.B., J.C.D., Incardination and Excardination of Seculars, XX-585 pp., 1941.
146. Król, Rev. John T., J.C.D., The Defendant in Contentious Trials, XII-207 pp., 1942.
147. Comyns, Rev. Joseph J., C.SS.R., A.B., J.C.D., Papal and Episcopal Administration of Church Property, XIV-155 pp., 1942.
148. Barry, Rev. Garrett Francis, O.M.I., J.C.D., Violation of the Cloister, XII-260 pp., 1942.
149. Bolduc, Rev. Gatien, C.S.V., A.B., S.T.L., J.C.D., Les Études dans les Religions Cléricales, VIII-155 pp., 1942.
150. Boyle, Rev. David John, M.A., J.C.D., The Juridic Effects of Moral Certitude on Pre-Nuptial Guarantees, XII-188 pp., 1942.
151. **Canavan, Rev. Walter Joseph, M.A., Litt.D., J.C.D., The Profes**sion of Faith, XII-143 pp., 1942.

152. DESROCHERS, REV. BRUNO, A.B., Ph.L., S.T.B., J.C.D., Le Premier Concile Plénier de Québec et le Code de Droit Canonique, XIV–186 pp., 1942.
153. DILLON, REV. ROBERT EDWARD, A.B., J.C.D., Common Law Marriage, X-148 pp., 1942.
154. DODWELL, REV. EDWARD JOHN, Ph.D., S.T.B., J.C.D., The Time and Place for the Celebration of Marriage, X-156 pp., 1942.
155. DONNELLAN, REV. THOMAS ANDREW, A.B., J.C.D., The Obligation of the Missa pro Populo, VII-131 pp., 1942.
156. ELTZ, REV. LOUIS ANTHONY, A.B., J.C.D., Cooperation in Crime, XII-208 pp., 1942.
157. GASS, REV. SYLVESTER FRANCIS, M.A., J.C.D., Ecclesiastical Pensions, XI-206 pp., 1942.
158. GUINIVEN, REV. JOHN JOSEPH, C.SS.R., J.C.D., The Precept of Hearing Mass, XIV-188 pp., 1942.
159. GULCZYNSKI, REV. JOHN THEOPHILUS, J.C.D., The Desecration and Violation of Churches, X-126 pp., 1942.
160. HAMMILL, REV. JOHN LEO, M.A., J.C.D., The Obligations of the Traveler According to Canon 14, VIII-204 pp., 1942.
161. HAYDT, REV. JOHN JOSEPH, A.B., J.C.D., Reserved Benefices, XI-148 pp., 1942.
162. HUSER, REV. ROGER JOHN, O.F.M., A.B., J.C.D., The Crime of Abortion in Canon Law, XII-187 pp., 1942.
163. KEARNEY, REV. FRANCIS PATRICK, A.B., S.T.L., J.C.D., The Principles of Canon 1127, X-162 pp., 1942.
164. LINAHEN, REV. LEO JAMES, S.T.L., J.C.D., De Absolutione Complicis In Peccato Turpi, 114 pp., 1942.
165. MCCLOSKEY, REV. JOSEPH ALOYSIUS, A.B., J.C.D., The Subject of Ecclesiastical Law According to Canon 12, XVII-246 pp., 1942.
166. O'NEILL, REV. FRANCIS JOSEPH, C.SS.R., J.C.D., The Dismissal of Religious in Temporary Vows, XIII-220 pp., 1942.
167. PRINCE, REV. JOHN EDWARD, A.B., S.T.B., J.C.D., The Diocesan Chancellor, X-136 pp., 1942.
168. RIESNER, REV. ALBERT JOSEPH, C.SS.R., J.C.D., Apostates and Fugitives from Religious Institutes, IX-168 pp., 1942.
169. STENGER, REV. JOSEPH BERNARD, J.C.D., The Mortgaging of Church Property, 186 pp., 1942.
170. WALDRON, REV. JOSEPH FRANCIS, A.B., J.C.D., The Minister of Baptism, XII-197 pp., 1942.
171. WILLETT, REV. ROBERT ALBERT, J.C.D., The Probative Value of Documents in Ecclesiastical Trials, X-124 pp., 1942.
172. WOEBER, REV. EDWARD MARTIN, M.A., J.C.D., The Interpellations, XII-161 pp., 1942.
173. BENKO, REV. MATTHEW ALOYSIUS, O.S.B., M.A., J.C.D., The Abbot *Nullius*, XIV-148 pp., 1943.

174. CHRIST, REV. JOSEPH JAMES, M.A., S.T.L., J.C.D., Dispensation from Vindicative Penalties, XIV-285 pp., 1943.
175. CLANCY, REV. PATRICK M. J., O.P., A.B., S.T.Lr., J.C.D., The Local Religious Superior, X-229 pp., 1943.
176. CLARKE, REV. THOMAS JAMES, J.C.D., Parish Societies, XII-147 pp., 1943.
177. CONNOLLY, REV. JOHN PATRICK, S.T.L., J.C.D., Synodal Examiners and Parish Priest Consultors, X-223 pp., 1943.
178. DRUMM, REV. WILLIAM MARTIN, A.B., J.C.D., Hospital Chaplains, XII-175 pp., 1943.
179. FLANAGAN, REV. BERNARD JOSEPH, A.B., S.T.L., J.C.D., The Canonical Erection of Religious Houses, X-147 pp., 1943.
180. KELLEHER, REV. STEPHEN JOSEPH, A.B., S.T.B., J.C.D., Discussions with Non-Catholics: Canonical Legislation, X-93 pp., 1943.
181. LEWIS, REV. GORDIAN, C.P., J.C.D., Chapters in Religious Institutes, XII-169 pp., 1943.
182. MARX, REV. ADOLPH, J.C.D., The Declaration of Nullity of Marriages Contracted Outside the Church, X-151 pp., 1943.
183. MATULENAS, REV. RAYMOND ANTHONY, O.S.B., A.B., J.C.D., Communication, a Source of Privileges, XII-225 pp., 1943.
184. O'LEARY, REV. CHARLES GERARD, C.SS.R., J.C.D., Religious Dismissed After Perpetual Profession, X-213 pp., 1943.
185. POWER, REV. CORNELIUS MICHAEL, J.C.D., The Blessing of Cemeteries, XII-231 pp., 1943.
186. SHUHLER, REV. RALPH VINCENT, O.S.A., J.C.D., Privileges of Regulars to Absolve and Dispense, XII-195 pp., 1943.
187. ZIOLKOWSKI, REV. THADDEUS STANISLAUS, A.B., J.C.D., The Consecration and Blessing of Churches, XII-151 pp., 1943.
188. HENEGHAN, REV. JOHN JOSEPH, S.T.D., J.C.D., The Marriages of Unworthy Catholics: Canons 1065 and 1066, XVI-213 pp., 1944.
189. CARROLL, REV. COLEMAN FRANCIS, M.A., S.T.L., J.C.L., Charitable Institutions.
190. CIESLUK, REV. JOSEPH EDWARD, Ph.B., S.T.L., J.C.L., National Parishes in the United States.
191. COBURN, REV. VINCENT PAUL, A.B., J.C.D., Marriages of Conscience, XII-172 pp., 1944.
192. CONNORS, REV. CHARLES PAUL, C.S.Sp., A.B., J.C.D., Extra-Judicial Procurators in the Code of Canon Law, X-94 pp., 1944.
193. COYLE, REV. PAUL RAYMOND, A.B., J.C.D., Judicial Exceptions, X-142 pp., 1944.
194. FAIR, REV. BARTHOLOMEW FRANCIS, A.B., S.T.L., J.C.L., The Impediment of Abduction.
195. GALLAGHER, REV. THOMAS RAPHAEL, O.P., A.B., S.T.Lr., J.C.D., The Examination of the Qualities of the Ordinand, X-166 pp., 1944.
196. GANNON, REV. JOHN MARK, S.T.L., J.C.D., The Interstices Required for the Promotion to Orders, XII-100 pp., 1944.

197. Goldsmith, Rev. J. William, B.C.S., S.T.L., J.C.D., The Competence of Church and State over Marriage—Disputed Points, X-128 pp., 1944.
198. Goodwine, Rev. Joseph Gerard, A.B., S.T.B., J.C.D., The Reception of Converts, XIV-326 pp., 1944.
199. Kowalski, Rev. Romuald Eugene, O.F.M., A.B., J.C.D., Sustenance of Religious Houses of Regulars, X-174 pp., 1944.
200. McCoy, Rev. Alan Edward, O.F.M., J.C.D., Force and Fear in Relation to Delictual Imputability and Penal Responsibility, XII-160 pp., 1944.
201. McDevitt, Rev. Vincent John, Ph.B., S.T.L., J.C.L., Perjury.
202. Martin, Rev. Thomas Owen, Ph.D., S.T.D., J.C.D., Adverse Possession, Prescription and Limitation of Actions: The Canonical "Praescriptio," XX-208 pp., 1944.
203. Miklosovic, Rev. Paul John, A.B., J.C.L., Attempted Marriages and Their Consequent Juridic Effects.
204. Mundy, Rev. Thomas Maurice, A.B., S.T.L., J.C.D., The Union of Parishes, X—164 pp., 1945.
205. O'Dea, Rev. John Coyle, A.B., J.C.D., The Matrimonial Impediment of Nonage, VIII-126 pp., 1944.
206. Olalia, Rev. Alexander Ayson, S.T.L., J.C.D., A Comparative Study of the Christian Constitution of States and the Constitution of the Philippine Commonwealth, XII—136 pp., 1944.
207. Poisson, Rev. Pierre-Marie, C.S.C., A.B., Ph.L., Th.L., J.C.L., Droits Patrimoniaux des Maisons et des Églises Religieuses.
208. Stadalnikas, Rev. Casimir Joseph, M.I.C., J.C.D., Reservation of Censures, X-141 pp., 1944.
209. Sullivan, Rev. Eugene Henry, S.T.L., J.C.D., Proof of the Reception of the Sacraments, X—165 pp., 1944.
210. Vaughan, Rev. William Edward, J.C.D., Constitutions for Diocesan Courts, X-210 pp., 1944.
211. Paro, Rev. Gino, S.T.D., J.C.L., The Right of Apostolic Legation.
212. Balzer, Rev. Ralph Francis, C.P., J.C.L., The Computation of Time in a Canonical Novitiate.
213. Dougherty, Rev. John Whelan, A.B., S.T.L., J.C.L., De Inquisitione Speciali.
214. Dziob, Rev. Michael Walter, J.C.L., The Sacred Congregation for the Oriental Church.
215. Eidenschink, Rev. John Albert, O.S.B., B.A., J.C.L., The Election of Bishops in the Letters of Pope Gregory the Great.
216. Gill, Rev. Nicholas, C.P., J.C.L., The Spiritual Prefect in Clerical Religious Houses of Study.

www.ingramcontent.com/pod-product-compliance
Lightning Source LLC
LaVergne TN
LVHW050213080826
844660LV00012B/405

* 9 7 8 0 8 1 3 2 2 4 0 0 8 *